PHONICS: GRADE 1
TABLE OF CONTENTS

PHONICS – GRADE 1

This book is designed to review phonics to enhance reading ability. The activities provide a fun way to reinforce daily learning and will keep skills sharp over an extended vacation as well as allow a child to gain an edge from extra practice.

ORGANIZATION

These activities are designed to reinforce skills that are important for beginning readers. This book is divided into four sections: *Recognizing Letters; Letters and Sounds: Consonants; Letters and Sounds: Short Vowels;* and *Letters and Sounds: Long Vowels*. Each section focuses on a single concept, and review pages appear periodically to give children the opportunity to review several familiar sounds while they work with unfamiliar sounds.

- **Recognizing Letters**. Because letter recognition is a review skill for most first graders, letters are reviewed in groups of three. On each page children will write the capital and lower-case letters, locate lower-case letters in words, and match partner letters.

- **Letters and Sounds: Consonants.** In this section, children will practice listening for and writing consonants in initial, medial, and final positions. The key picture at the top of each page can be used to remind the student of the letter's sound as he/she works through the activities.

- **Letters and Sounds: Short Vowels.** The activities in this section will help children recognize the short sounds vowels represent. Children will progress from listening for and writing short vowels to identifying rhyming words and reading sentences and stories with short vowel words.

- **Letters and Sounds: Long Vowels.** The activities for long vowels follow the same pattern as the short vowel pages, but the different spellings for each sound are introduced on individual pages.

USE

This book is designed for independent use by students who have been introduced to letters and sounds. Copies of the activities can be given to individuals, pairs of students, or small groups for completion. They may be used as a center activity. If students are familiar with the content, the worksheets can also be used as homework.

To begin, determine the implementation which fits your students' needs and your classroom structure. The following plan suggests a format for this implementation:

1. **Explain** the purpose of the worksheets to your class. Let students know that these activities will be fun as well as helpful.

2. **Review** the mechanics of how you want students to work with the activities. Do you want them to work in groups? Are these activities for homework?

3. **Introduce** students to the process and to the purpose of the activities. Go over the directions. Work with children when they have difficulty. Work only a few pages at a time to avoid pressure.

4. **Do** a practice activity together.

ADDITIONAL NOTES

1. **Parent Communication**. Send the Letter to Parents home with students.

2. **Bulletin Board**. Display completed activities to show student progress.

3. **Flashcards**. Use the colorful picture/letter cards to review and strengthen the student's skills. Supplement written activities with hands-on picture/letter card activities. The pictures on the cards are the same key pictures children use to recall the sound of each letter as they complete the activities.

4. **By ME! Books**. There are four child-sized books for children to make. Have children color the illustrations and complete the activity. To turn the page into a book, children first fold the page in the middle. Then they fold it again, making sure the cover is on top.

5. **Assessment**. Following the introduction is a two-page test. You can use the test as a diagnostic tool by administering it before children begin the activities. After children have completed the workbook, let them retake it to see the progress they have made.

6. **Center Activities**. Use the worksheets and flashcards as center activities to give students the opportunity to work cooperatively.

7. **Have fun**. Working with these activities can be fun as well as meaningful for you and your students.

Dear Parent,

During this school year, our class will be learning phonics to prepare for reading. We will be completing activity sheets that provide practice with these reading readiness skills. Learning to read can be stressful. By working together to prepare the students, we can reduce their stress level and help them learn that reading is fun.

From time to time, I may send home activity sheets. To best help your child, please consider the following suggestions:

- Provide a quiet place to work.
- Go over the directions together.
- Encourage your child to do his or her best.
- Check the lesson when it is complete.
- Go over your child's work, and note improvements as well as problems.

Help your child maintain a positive attitude about the activities. Let your child know that each lesson provides an opportunity to have fun and to learn. Above all, enjoy this time you spend with your child. As your child's ability to read develops, he or she will feel your support.

Thank you for your help!

Cordially,

Name ______________________________ Date ______________________

Write the letters that stand for the missing sounds.

 ___e___e___	 ___ea___	 ___a___
 ___o___	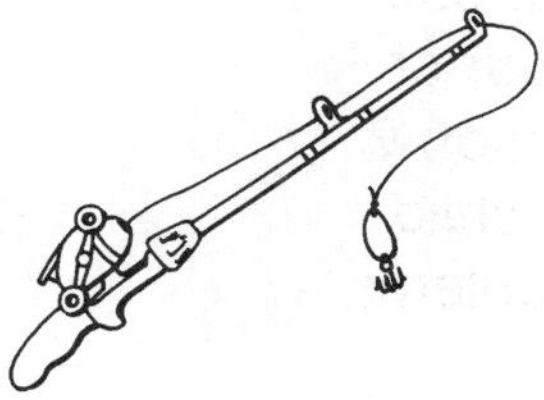 ___o___	 ___u___
 ___e___	 ___i___e	 ___a___

Name ______________________ Date ________________

Circle the letter or letters that stand for the vowel sound in the picture name.

 u u_e a_e	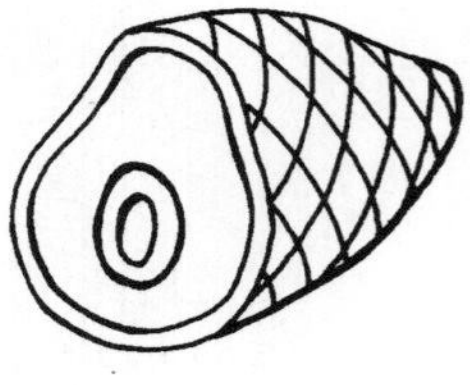 a ai e	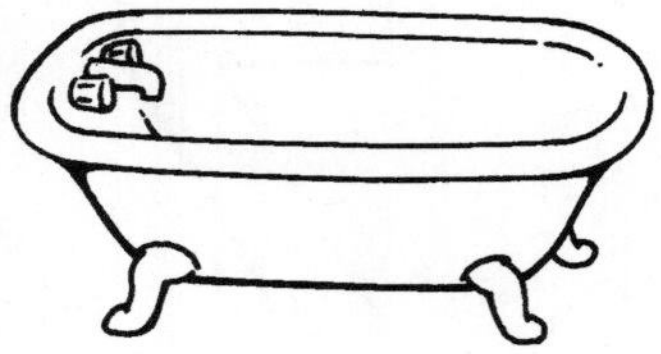 ee u_e u
 ai ee e	 e i_e ea	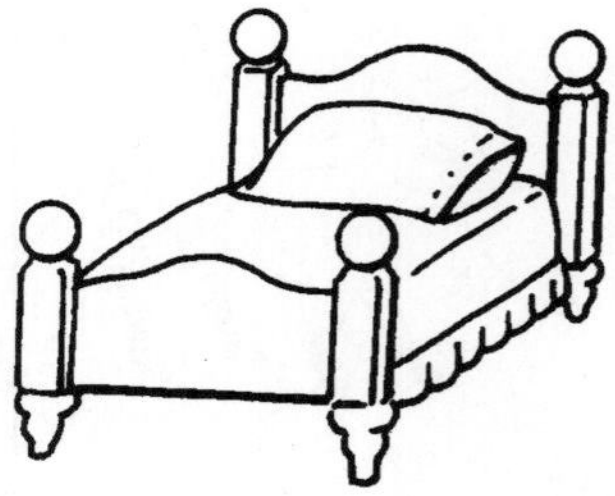 e u_e ee
 a oa ee	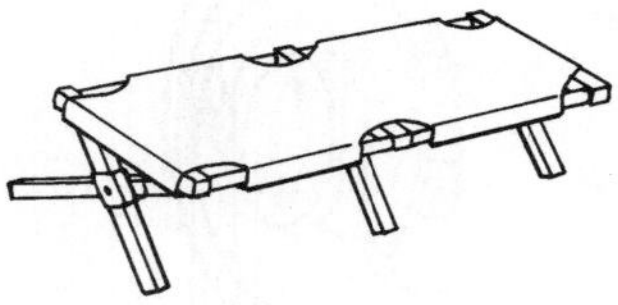 u o i	 i i_e a

Name ______________________ Date ______________

Write the letters that stand for the missing sounds.

 seven	 leaf	 hat
 fox	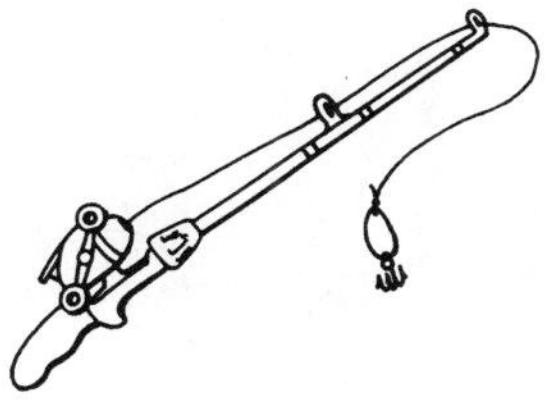 rod	 bug
 web	 dime	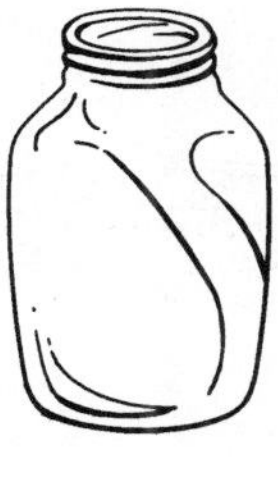 jar

Name ______________________ Date ______________

Circle the letter or letters that stand for the vowel sound in the picture name.

 u u_e a_e	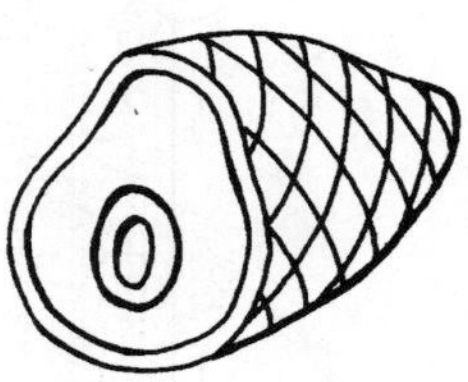 a ai e	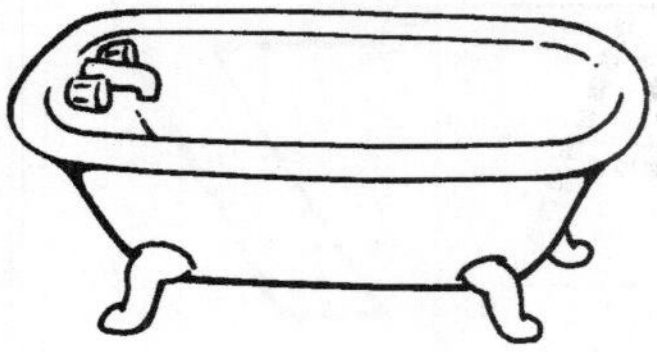 ee u_e u
 ai ee e	 e i_e ea	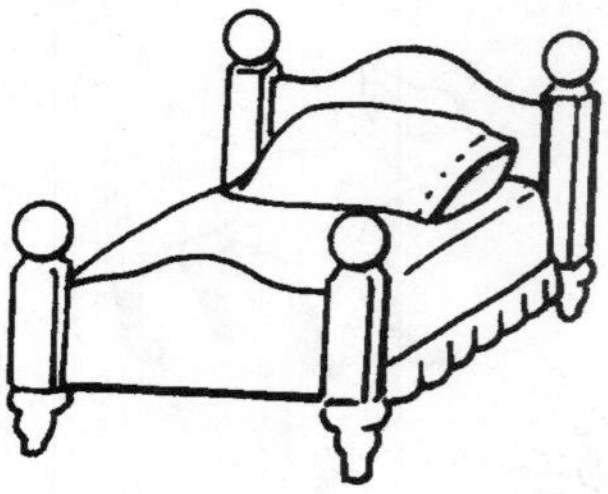 e u_e ee
 a oa ee	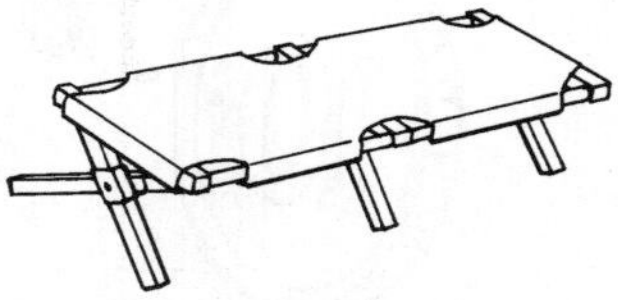 u o i	 i i_e a

Name________________________ Date________________

Write and Find Aa, Bb, Cc

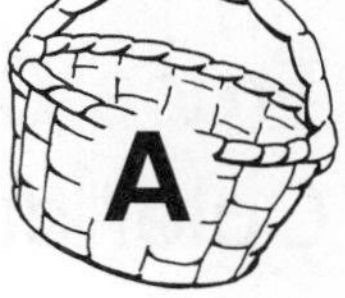

Trace **Aa**, **Bb**, and **Cc**. Write the letters on the lines. Color baskets with the same letter the same color.

A B C

a b c

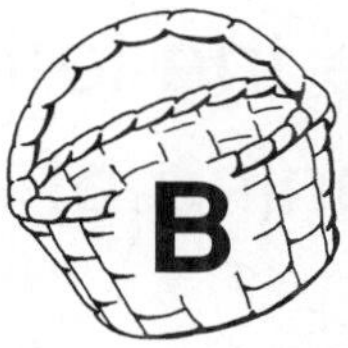

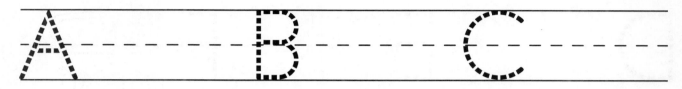

Circle the letters that match the letter at the beginning of each row.

ax **pan** **cat**

big **job** **baby**

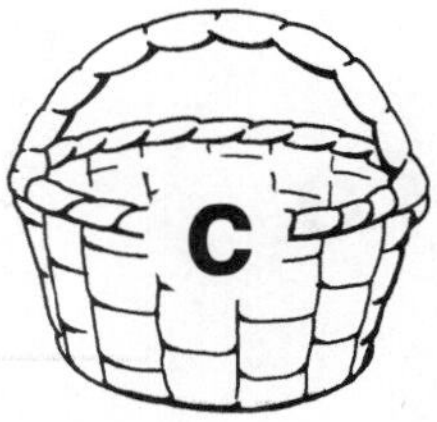

cat **face** **pack**

Name ______________________ Date ________________

Write and Find Dd, Ee, Ff

Trace **Dd**, **Ee**, and **Ff**. Write the letters on the lines. Color ducks with the same letter the same color.

D E F

d e f

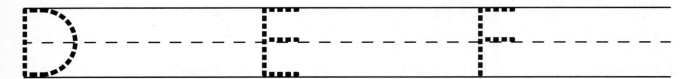

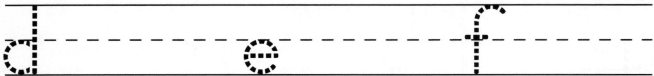

Circle the letters that match the letter at the beginning of each row.

dog **good** **dad**

egg **see** **red**

fun **leaf** **life**

Name ______________________ Date ________________

Write and Find Gg, Hh, Ii

Trace **Gg**, **Hh**, and **Ii**. Write the letters on the lines. Color hats with the same letter the same color.

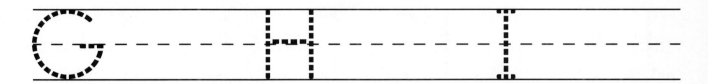

G H I

g h i

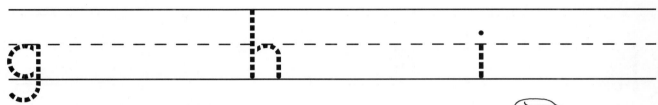

Circle the letters that match the letter at the beginning of each row.

gate soggy log

hill ashes arch

is dig inch

Name ______________________ Date ________________

Write and Find Jj, Kk, Ll

Trace **Jj**, **Kk**, and **Ll**. Write the letters on the lines.
Color jeeps with the same letter the same color.

J K L

j k l

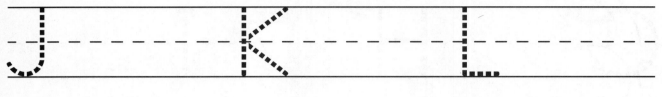

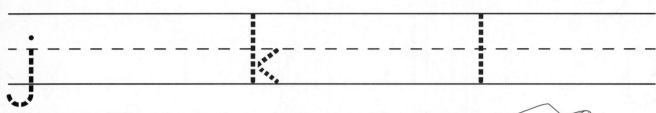

Circle the letters that match the letter at the beginning of each row.

jog jet jar

kick rake kite

hill leaf milk

Name ______________________ Date ________________

Traffic Jam

Color the cars that have partner letters on their wheels.

Name ______________________ Date ______________________

Write and Find Mm, Nn, Oo

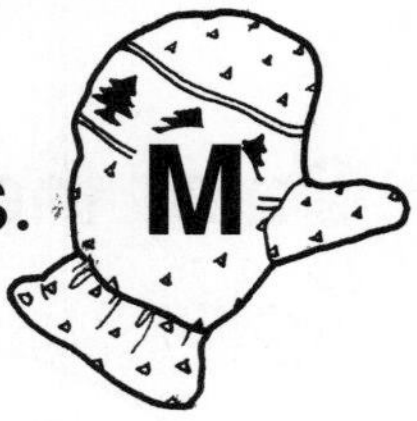

Trace **Mm**, **Nn**, and **Oo**. Write the letters on the lines. Color mittens with the same letter the same color.

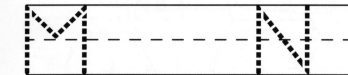

M N O

m n o

Circle the letters that match the letter at the beginning of each row.

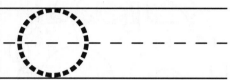

mom map ham

not fun nine

off hop too

Name ____________________ Date ____________

Write and Find Pp, Qq, Rr

Trace **Pp**, **Qq**, and **Rr**. Write the letters on the lines.
Color purses with the same letter the same color.

P Q R

p q r

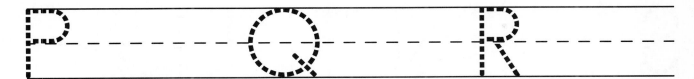

Circle the letters that match the letter at the beginning of each row.

pop shape nap

quack quit quilt

run purr where

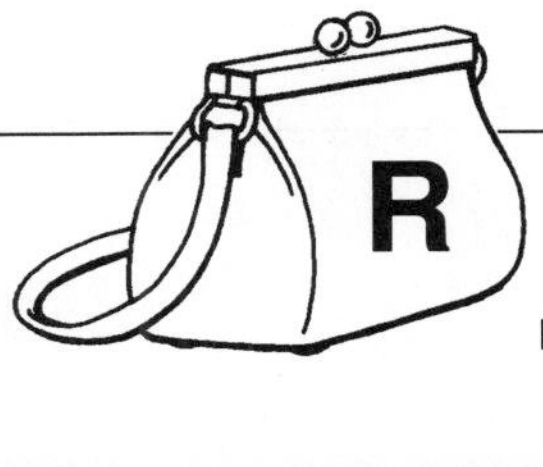

Name ____________________ Date ____________________

Write and Find Ss, Tt, Uu

Trace **Ss**, **Tt**, and **Uu**. Write the letters on the lines. Color suns with the same letter the same color.

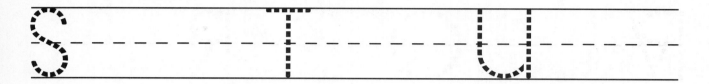

S T U

s t u

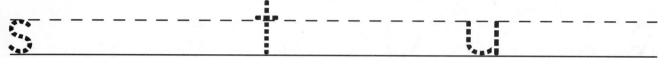

Circle the letters that match the letter at the beginning of each row.

seas sun dress

tent note two

nut us pup

Name ______________________ Date ________________

Write and Find Vv, Ww, Xx

Trace **Vv**, **Ww**, and **Xx**. Write the letters on the lines. Color watches with the same letter the same color.

V W X

v w x

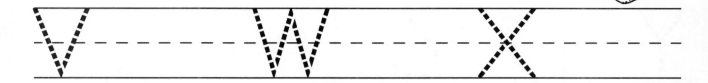

Circle the letters that match the letter at the beginning of each row.

van **love** **vet**

new **was** **two**

fox **ax** **mix**

Name ______________________ Date ________________

Write and Find Yy, Zz

Trace **Yy** and **Zz**. Write the letters on the lines.
Color yo-yos with the same letter the same color.

Y Z

y z

Circle the letters that match the letter at the beginning of each row.

yes	toys	you

maze	zoo	buzz

Name ______________________________ Date ______________________

Terrific Turtles

Color the turtles that have partner letters on their shells.

Name ______________________ Date ______________________

Alphabet Puzzle

Cut out the puzzle pieces. Put them together so the letters are in abc order.

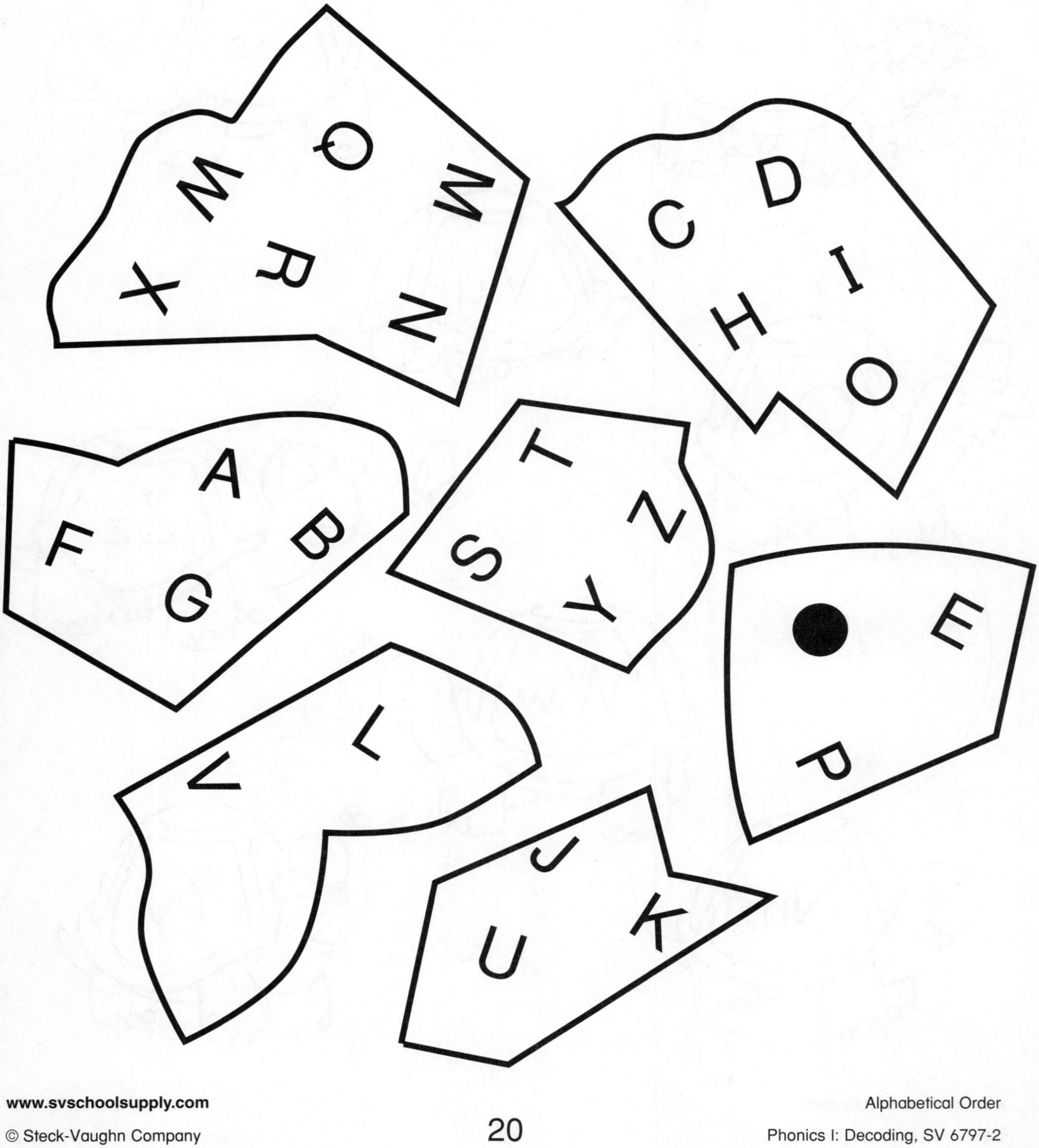

Name ______________________ Date ________________

Summer Swim

Help the frog find the pond. Draw lines from **A** to **L** in abc order.

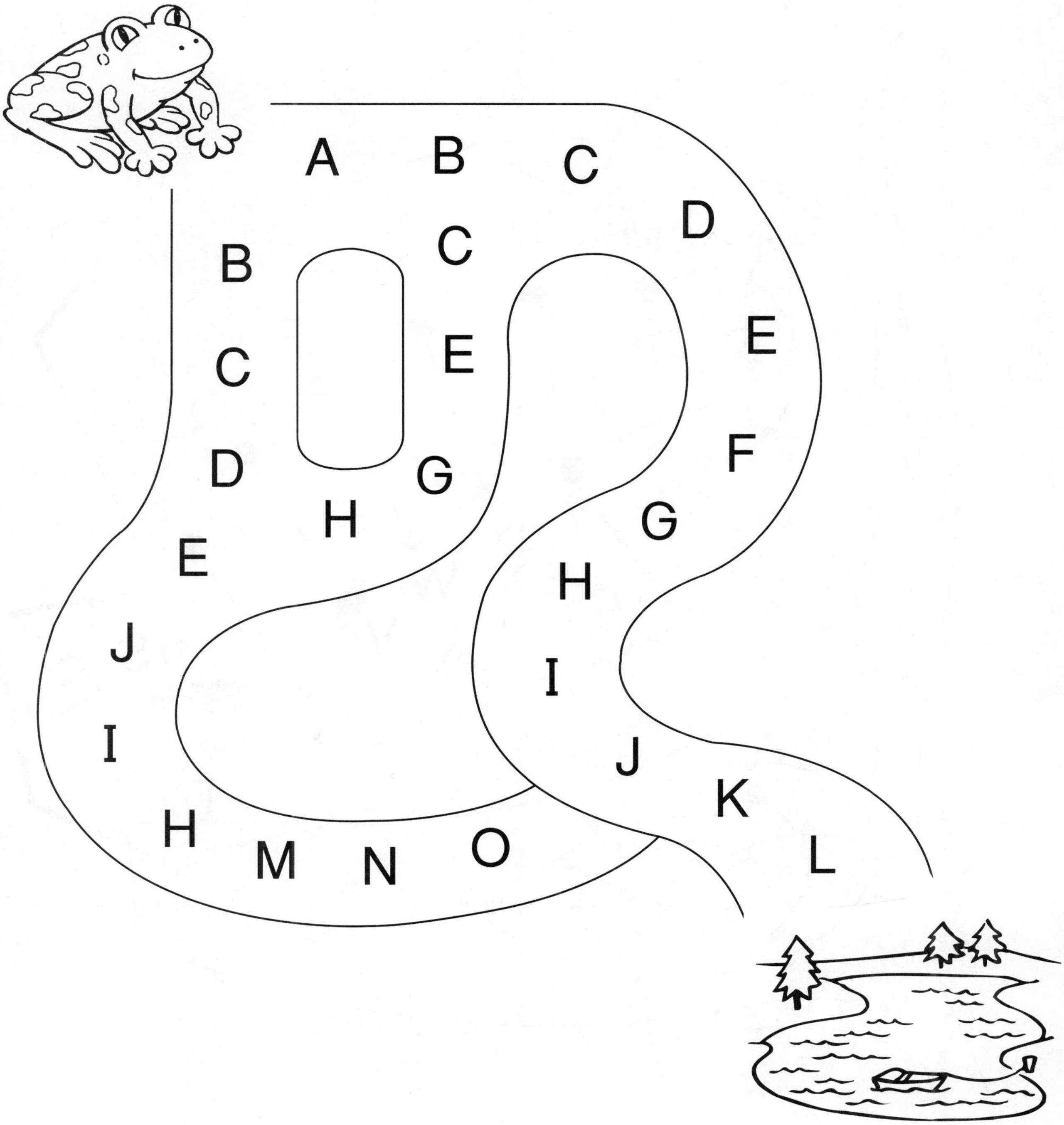

Name ______________________ Date ________________

What Is Hiding?

Find out what is hiding on the leaf. Draw lines from **M** to **Z** in abc order. Color the picture.

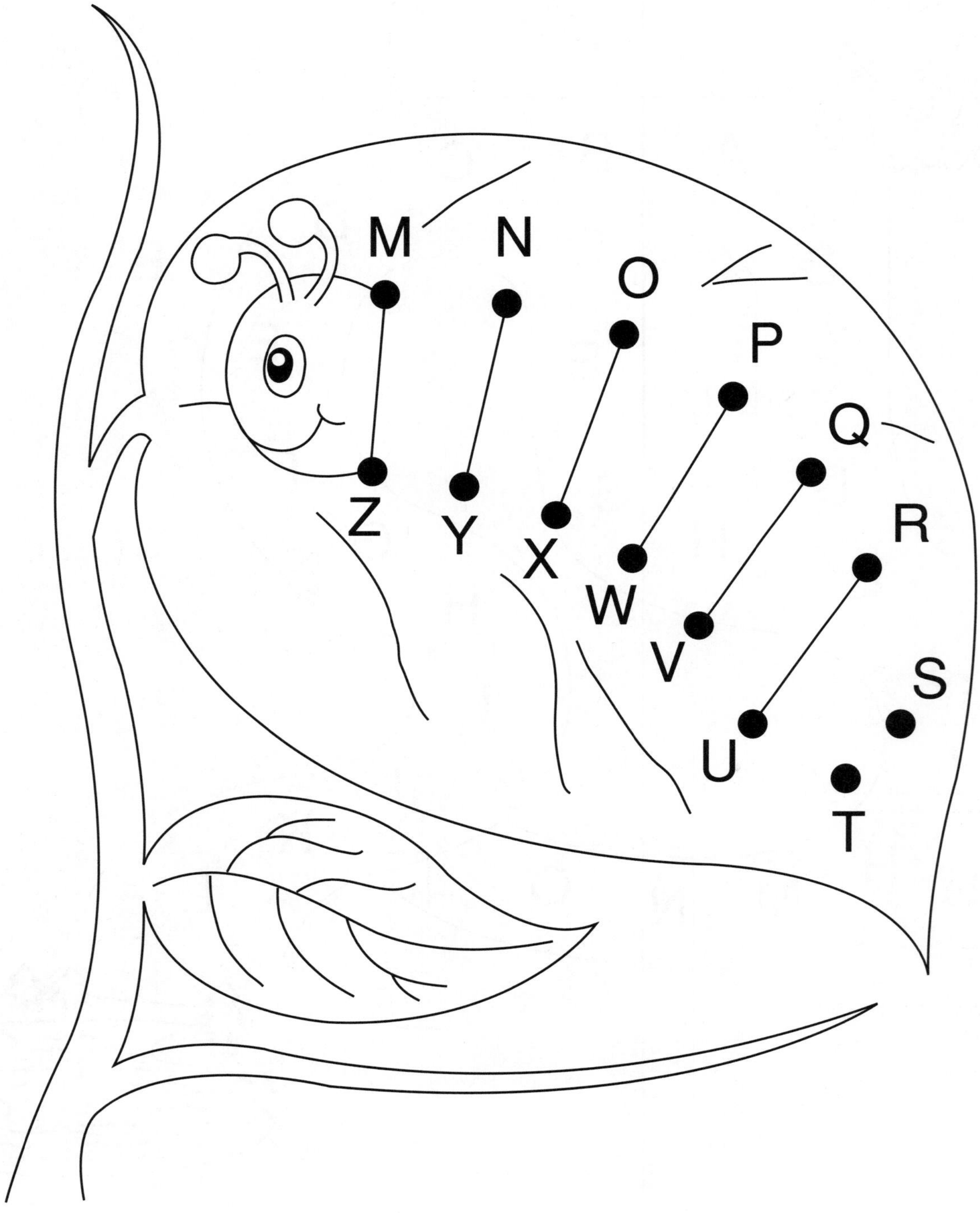

Fill in the missing letters
of the alphabet.

E F __ H

A B __ D

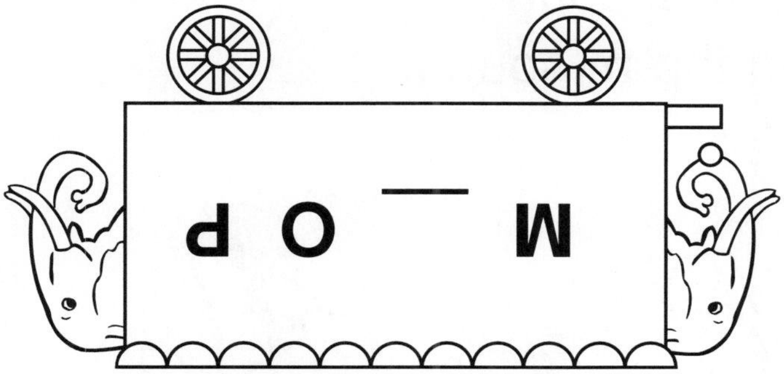

M __ O P

I J K __

Q R __ T

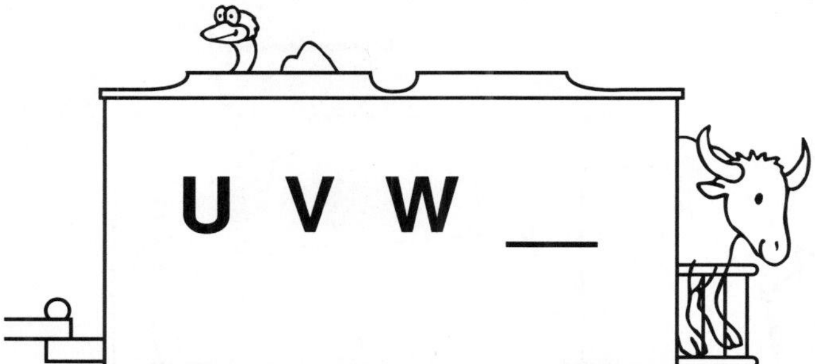

U V W __

Y Z

Alphabet Zoo Train

____

made this book!

Name ______________________ Date ____________________

The Sound of m

Name each picture. Listen to the first sound.
Color the pictures that begin with the **m** sound.

Name ____________________ Date ____________

Missing m 

Name each picture. If **m** stands for the missing sound, write **m** on the line.

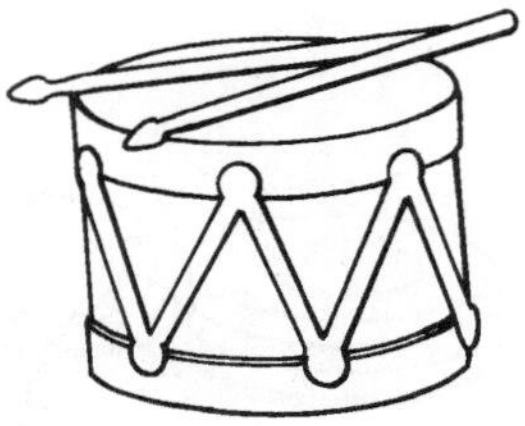 dru___	 ca___el	 lea___
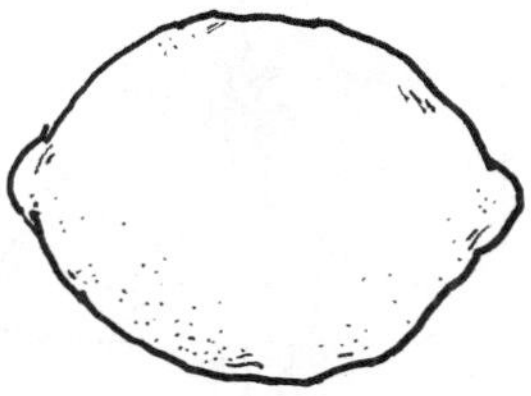 le___on	 ti___er	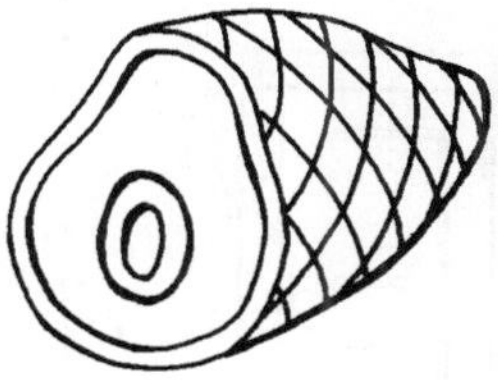 ha___
 sa___ad	 wo___an	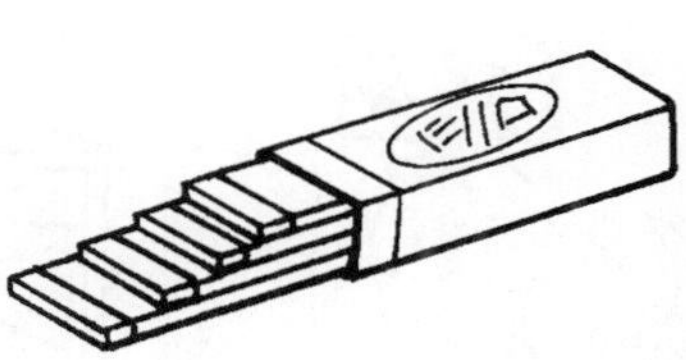 gu___

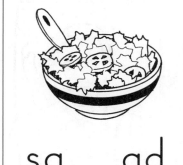

Name ______________________ Date ____________________

The Sound of d

Name each picture. Listen to the first sound.
If the name begins with the **d** sound, write **d**.

___

___

___

___

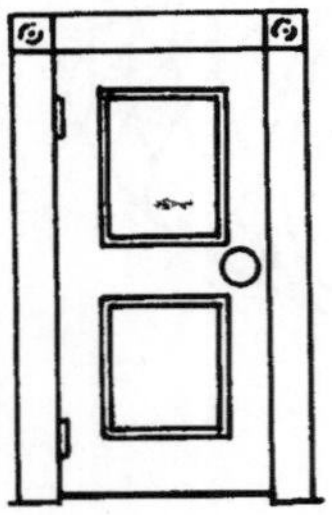

___

___

___

___

___

___

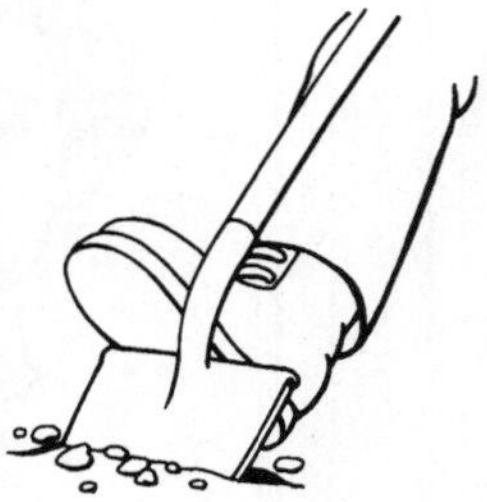

___

___

Name ______________________________ Date ______________________

Missing d

Name each picture. If **d** stands for the missing sound, write **d** on the line.

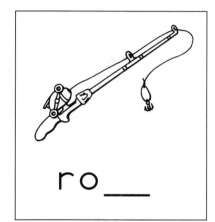

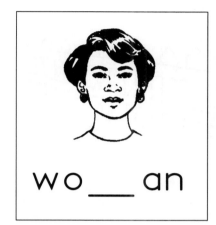

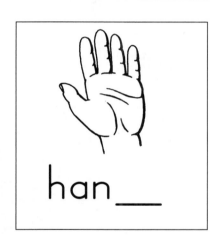

be___

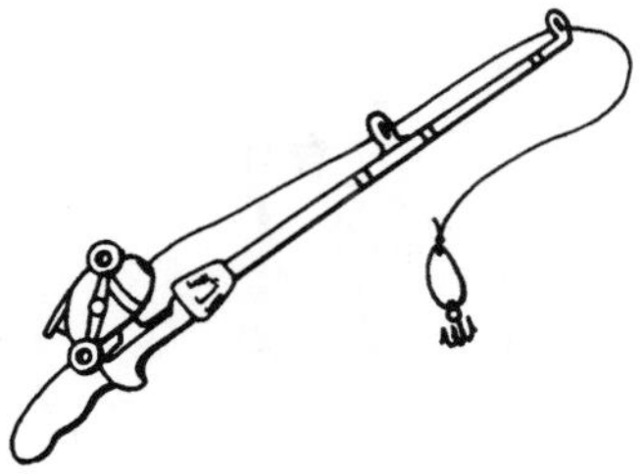

ro___

wo___an

ca___el

han___

ha___

me___al

spi___er

da___

Name______________________________ Date______________________

The Sound of f 

Name each picture. Listen to the first sound.
Color the pictures that begin with the **f** sound.

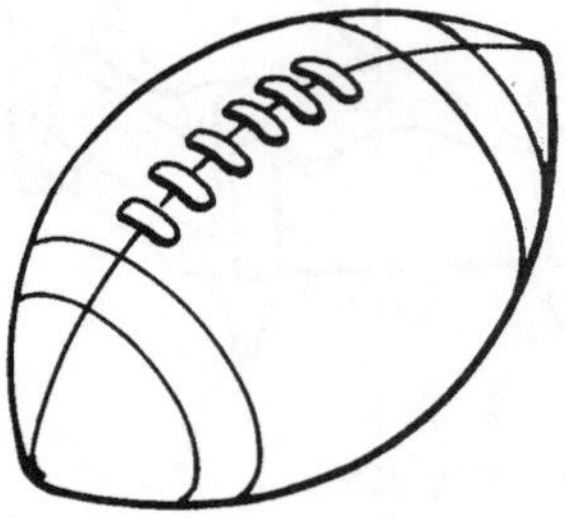

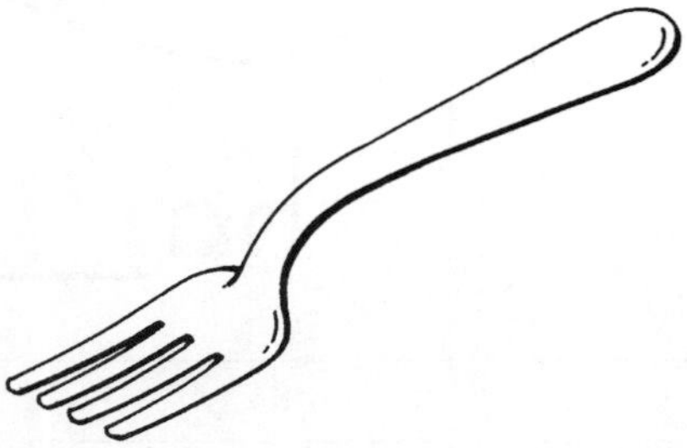

Name ______________________ Date ______________________

Missing f 

Name each picture. If **f** stands for the missing sound, write **f** on the line.

 el____	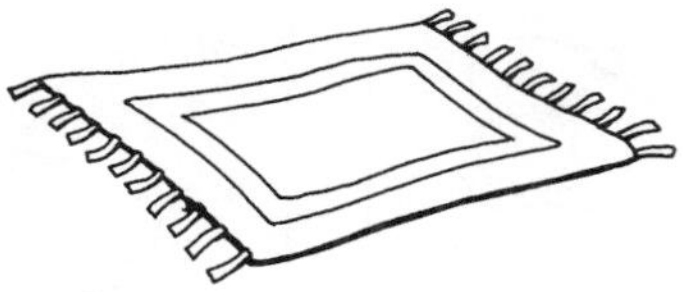 ru____	 roo____
 mo____	 hal____	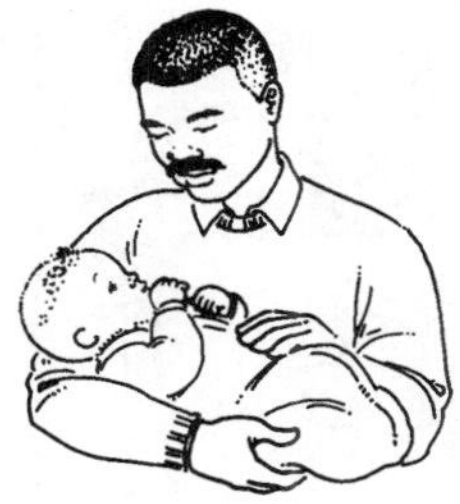 da____
 do____	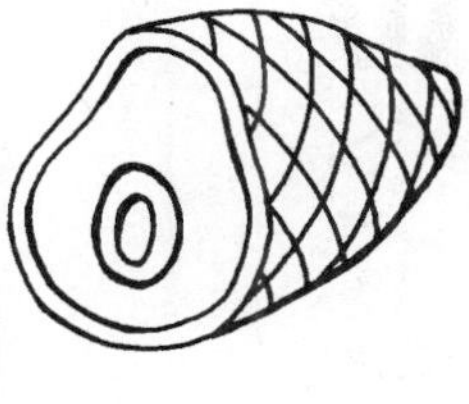 ha____	 lea____

Name ____________________ Date ____________________

The Sound of g 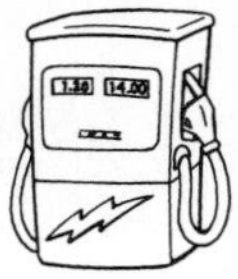

Name each picture. Listen to the first sound.
If the name begins with the **g** sound, write **g**.

 ___	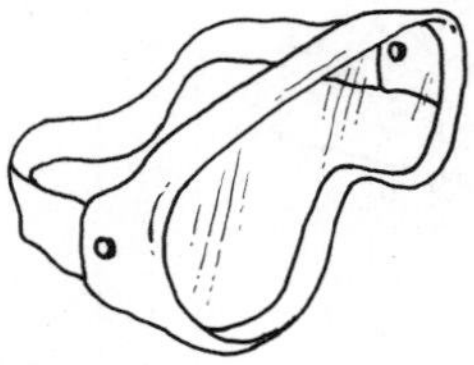 ___	 ___	 ___
 ___	 ___	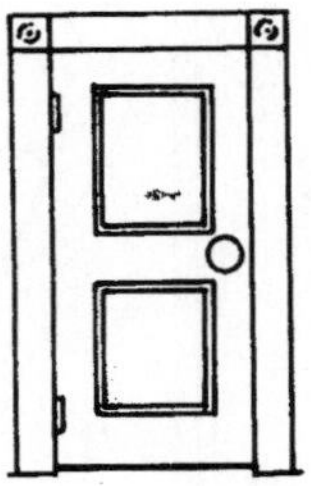 ___	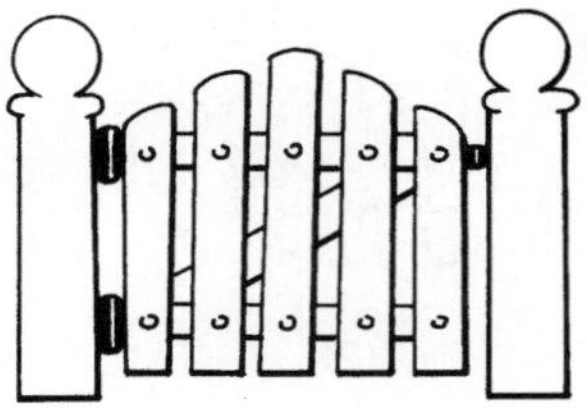 ___
 ___	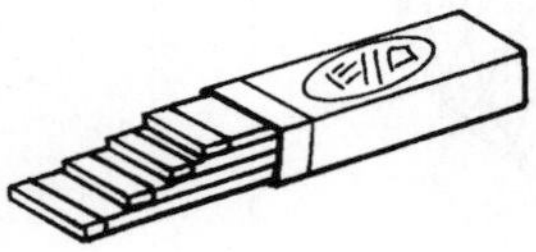 ___	 ___	 ___

Name ______________________________ Date ______________________

Missing g 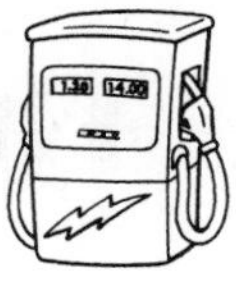

Name each picture. If **g** stands for the missing sound, write **g** on the line.

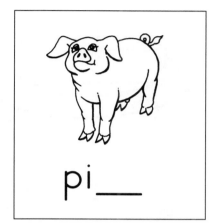

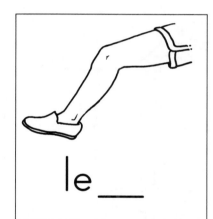

 wa___ on	 pi___	 ba___
 be___	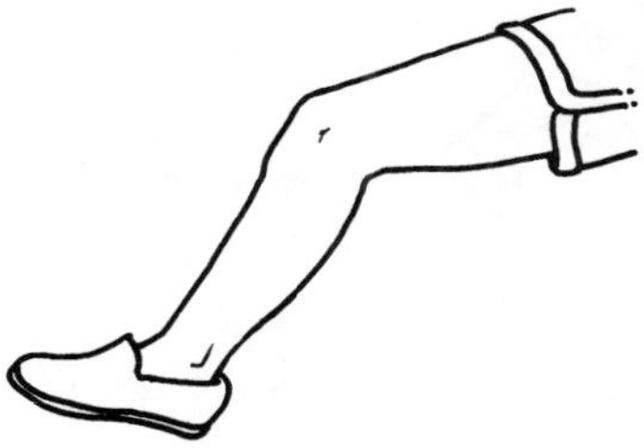 le___	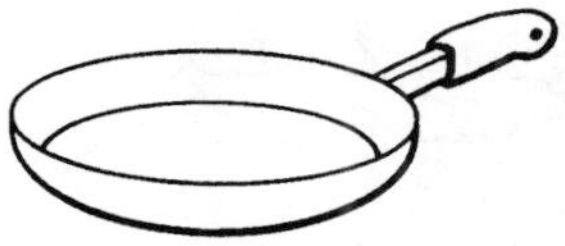 pa___
 do___ s	 bu___	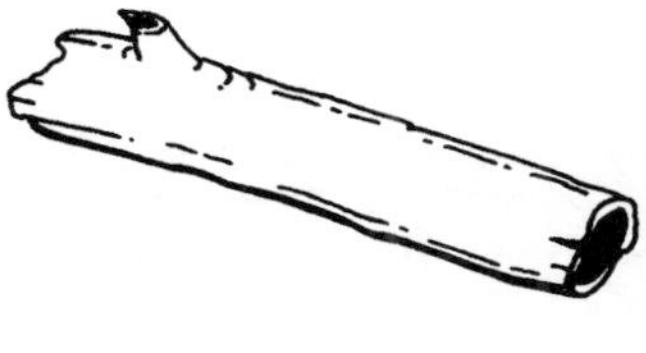 lo___

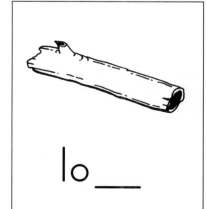

Name ______________________ Date ______________________

The Sound of b 

Name each picture. Listen to the first sound.
Color the pictures that begin with the **b** sound.

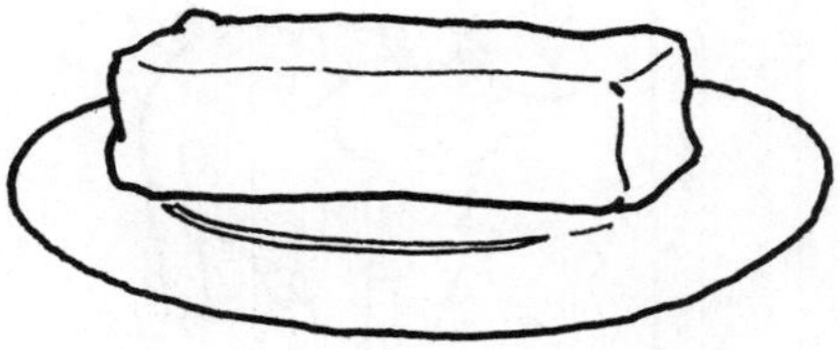

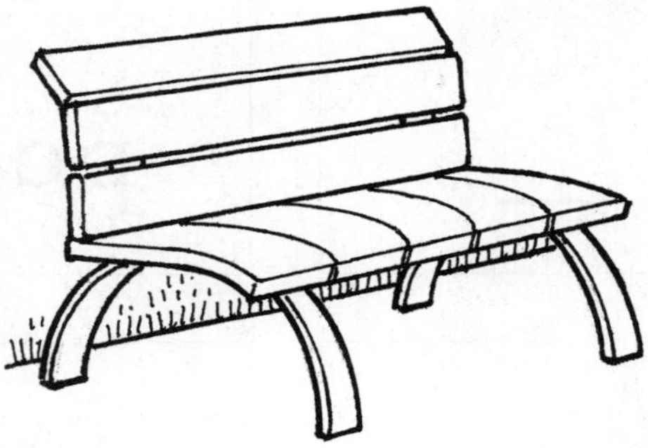

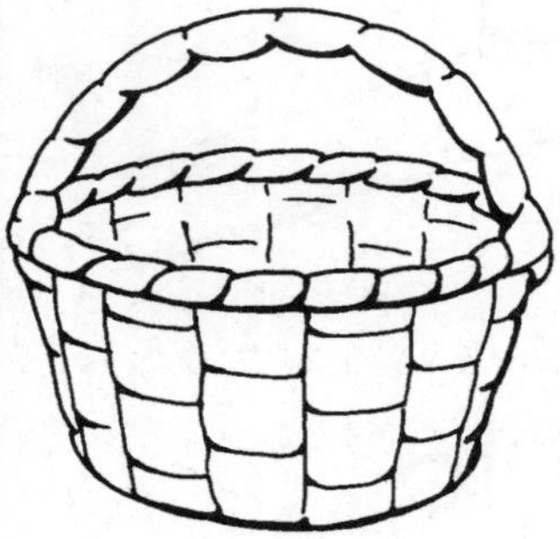

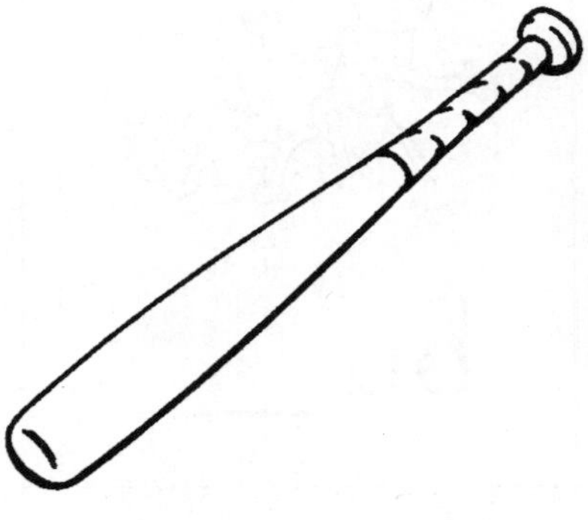

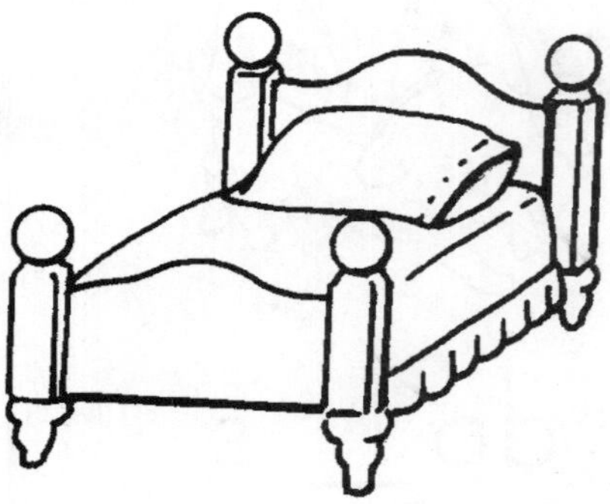

Name ______________________________ Date ______________________

Missing b 

Name each picture. If **b** stands for the missing sound, write **b** on the line.

we___

ca___in

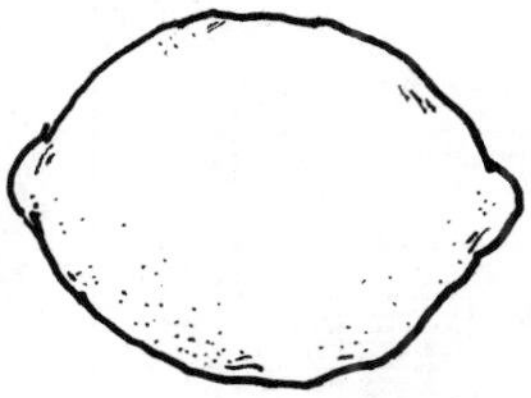

le___on

ro___ot

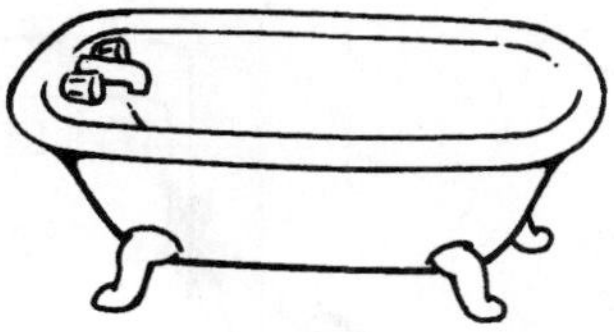

tu___

cu___

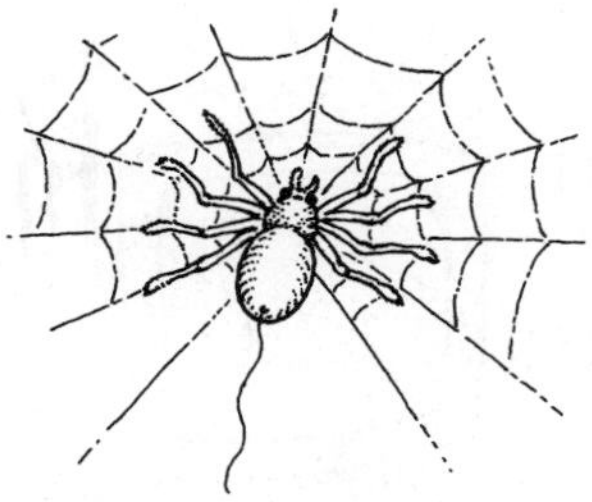

spi___er

bi___

ro___in

Name ______________________________ Date ______________________

The Sound of t 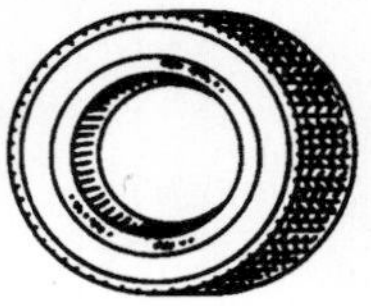

Name each picture. Listen to the first sound.
If the name begins with the **t** sound, write **t**.

 ___	 ___	 ___	 ___
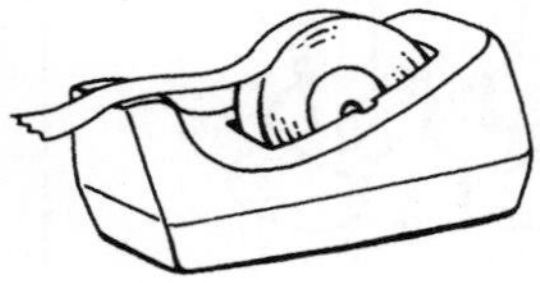 ___	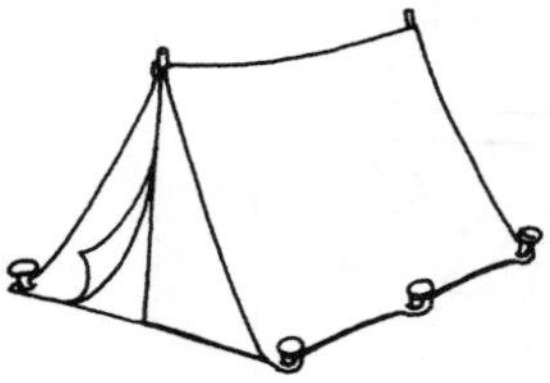 ___	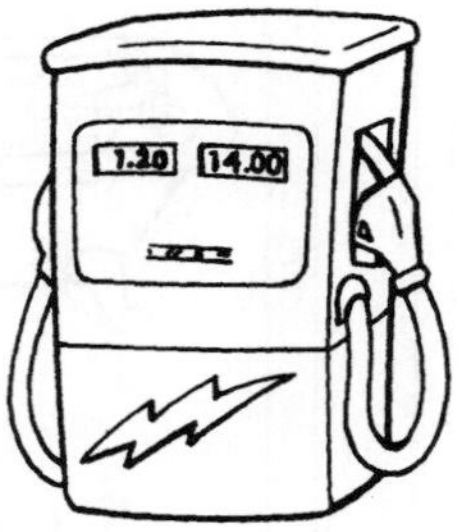 ___	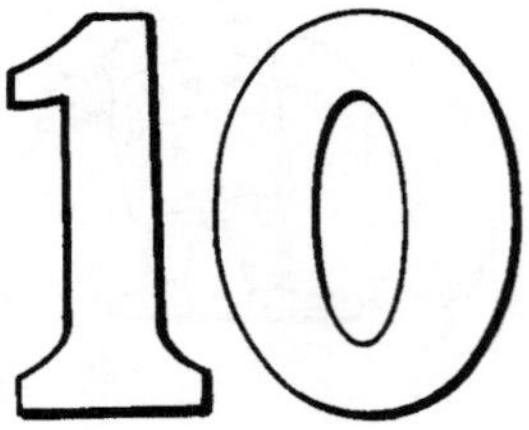 ___
 ___	 ___	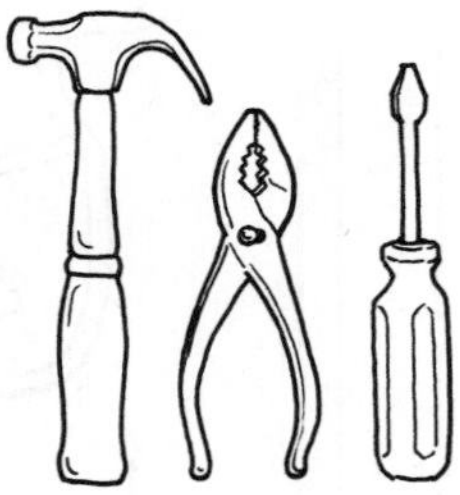 ___	 ___

Name ______________________ Date ________________

Missing t 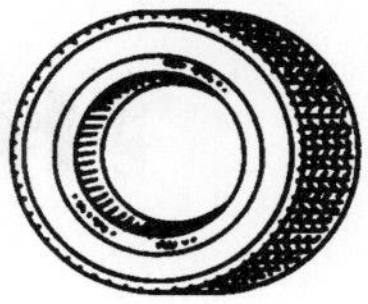

Name each picture. If **t** stands for the missing sound, write **t** on the line.

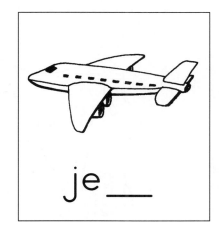

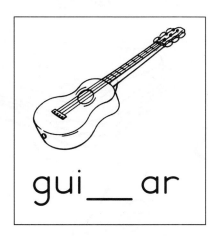

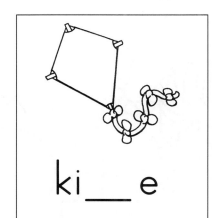

wa__ er

je__

ca__ in

gui__ ar

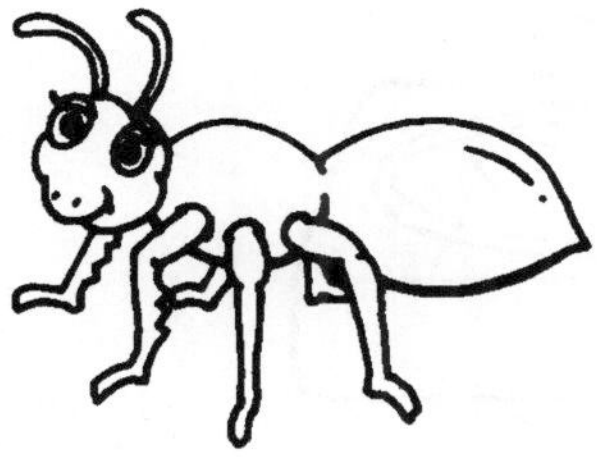

an__

ha__

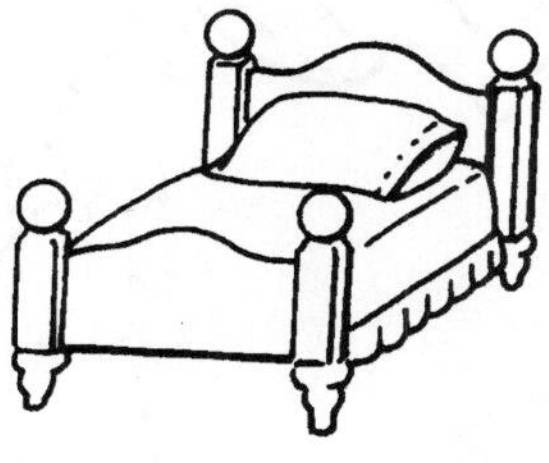

be__

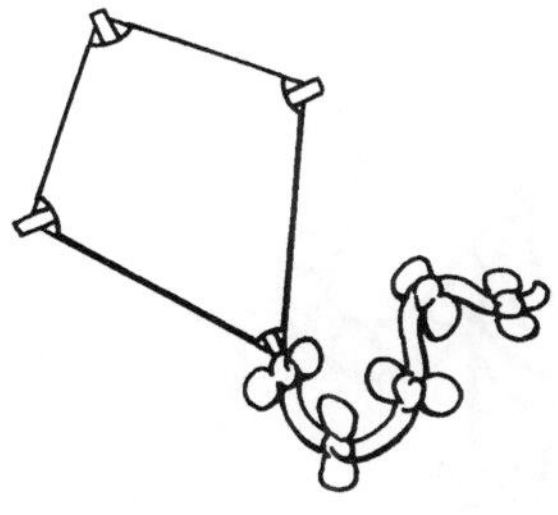

ki__ e

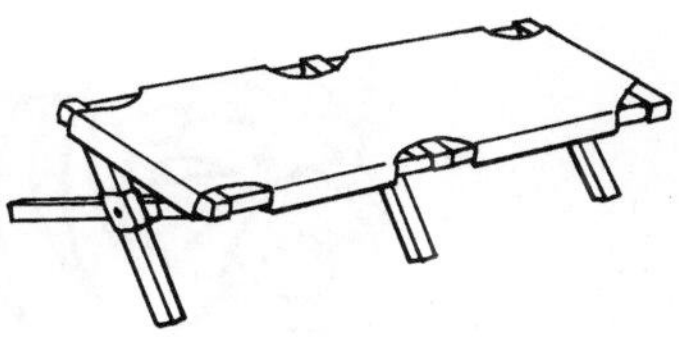

co__

Name ______________________________ Date ______________________

The Sound of s

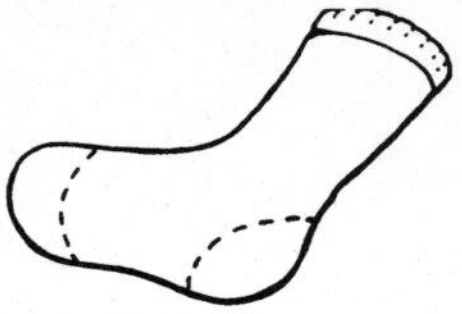

Name each picture. Listen to the first sound.
Color the pictures that begin with the **s** sound.

Name ______________________________ Date ______________________

Missing s

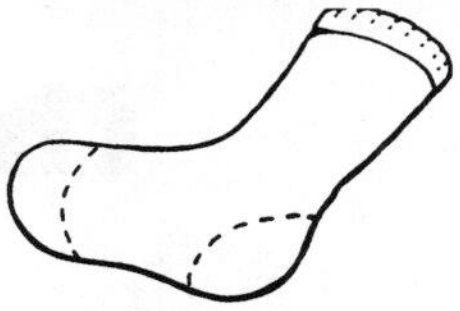

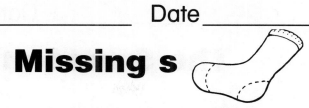

Name each picture. If **s** stands for the missing sound, write **s** on the line.

bu___

po___

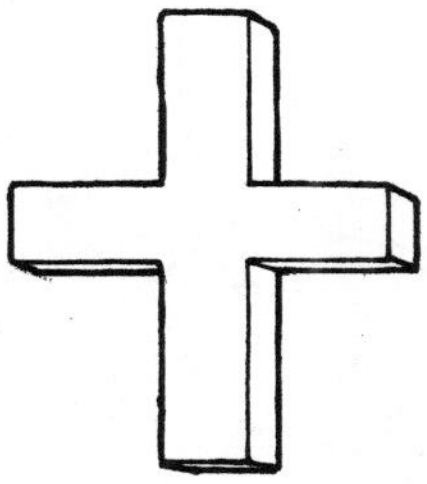

plu___

bi___

cactu___

robo___

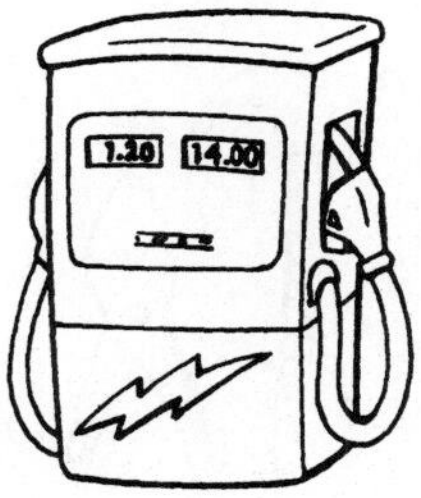

ga___

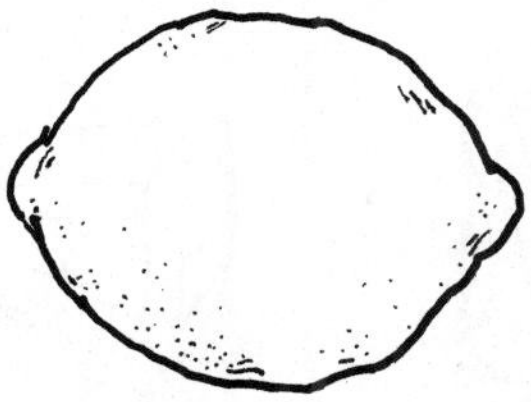

lemo___

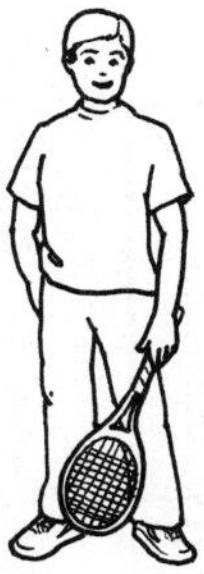

tenni___

Name ______________________ Date ________________

The Sound of w 

Name each picture. Listen to the first sound.
If the name begins with the **w** sound, write **w**.

 ____	 ____	 ____	 ____
 ____	 ____	 ____	 ____
 ____	 ____	 ____	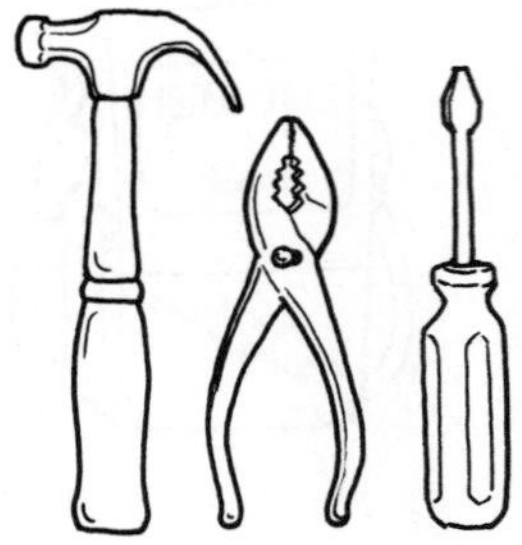 ____

Name ______________________ Date ________________

The Sound of k

Name each picture. Listen to the first sound.
Color the pictures that begin with the **k** sound.

Name ______________________ Date ________________

Missing k

Name each picture. If **k** stands for the missing sound, write **k** on the line.

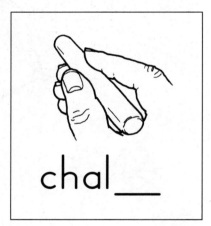

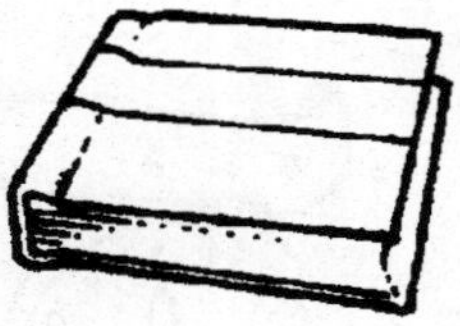

boo___

tur___ey

gui___ar

da___

for___

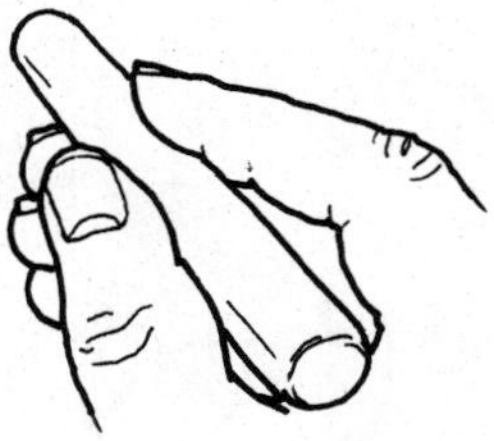

chal___

mil___

mon___ey

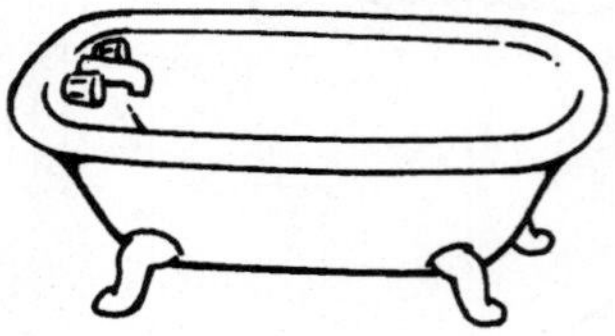

tu___

Name ______________________________ Date ______________________

The Sound of j 

Name each picture. Listen to the first sound.
If the name begins with the **j** sound, write **j**.

 ____	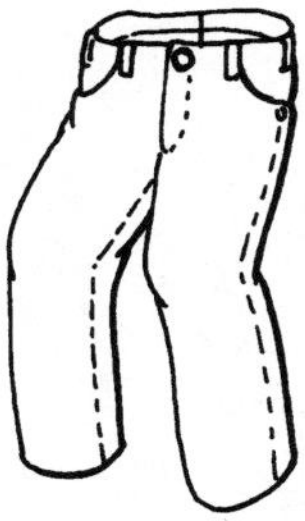 ____	 ____	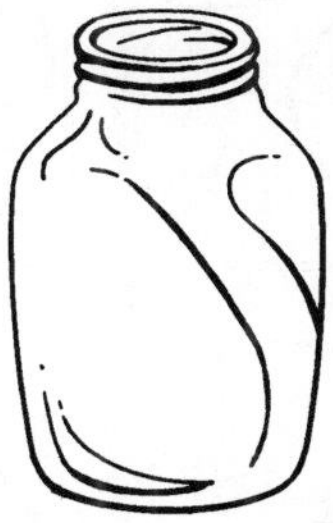 ____
 ____	 ____	 ____	 ____
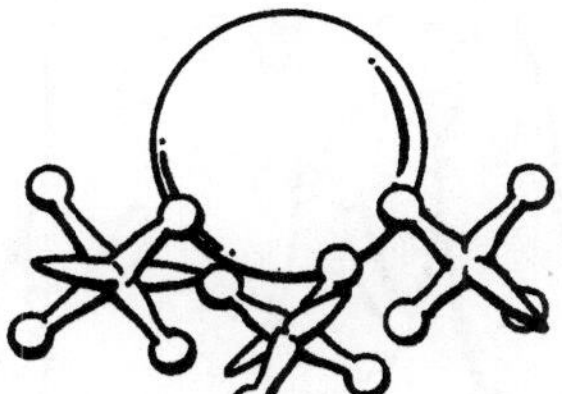 ____	 ____	 ____	 ____

Name ______________________ Date ________________

The Sound of p

Name each picture. Listen to the first sound.
Color the pictures that begin with the **p** sound.

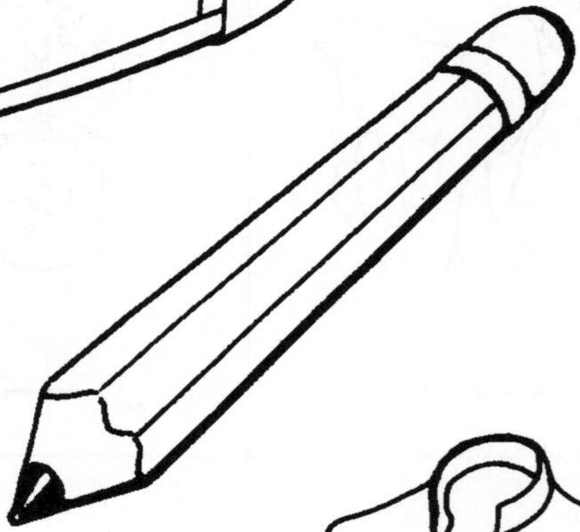

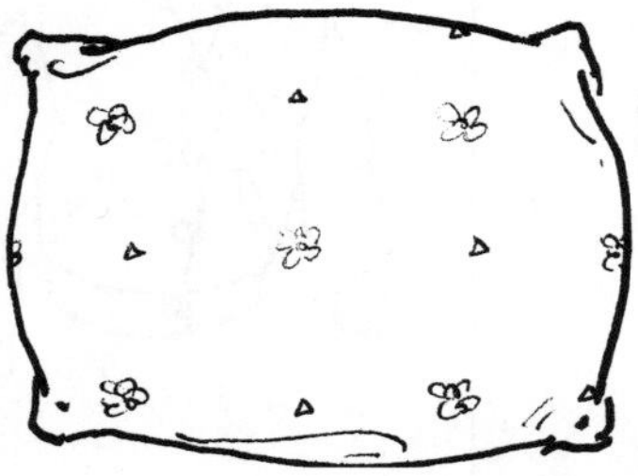

Name ______________________________ Date ______________________

Missing p

Name each picture. If **p** stands for the missing sound, write **p** on the line.

wi___er

ca___in

jee___

lea___

shi___

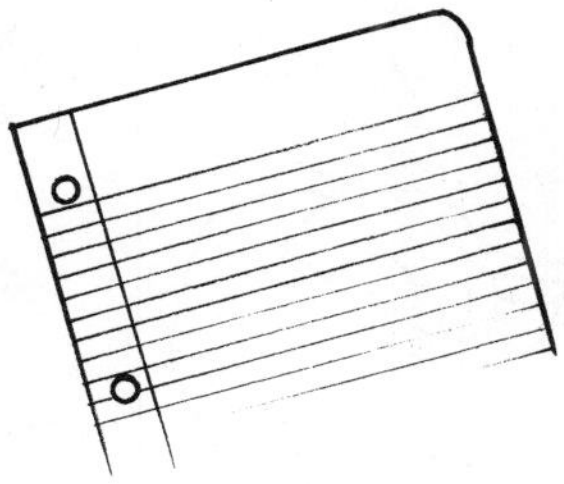

pa___er

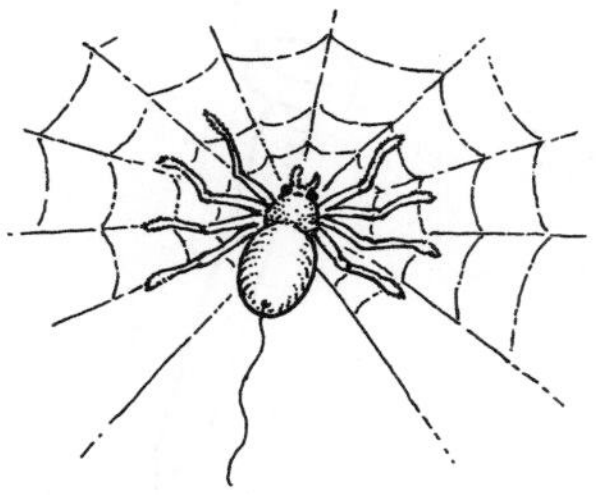

spi___er

mo___

do___

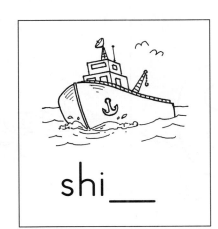

Name ______________________ Date ________________

The Sound of n 

Name each picture. Listen to the first sound.
If the name begins with the **n** sound, write **n**.

 ___	 ___	 ___	 ___
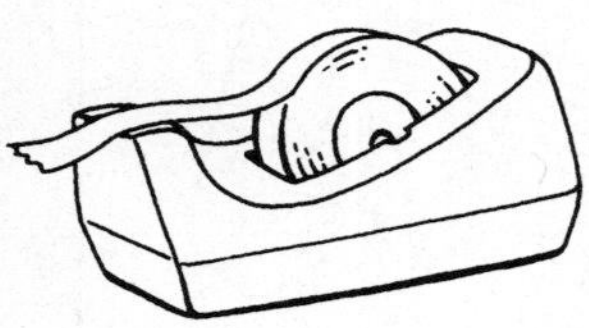 ___	 ___	 ___	 ___
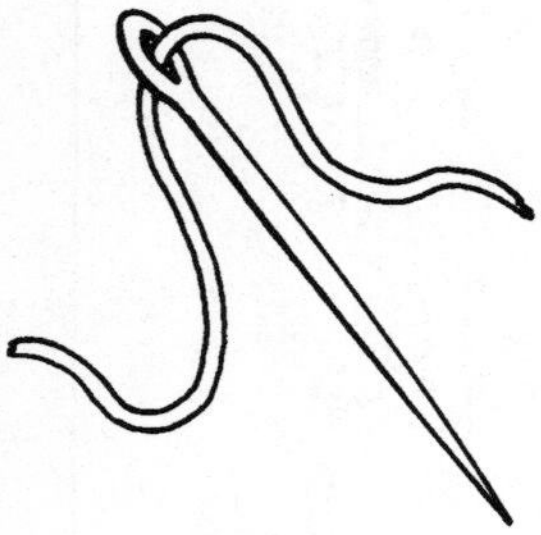 ___	 ___	 ___	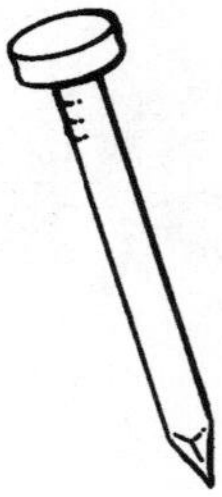 ___

Name ______________________ Date ________________

Missing n 

Name each picture. If **n** stands for the missing sound, write **n** on the line.

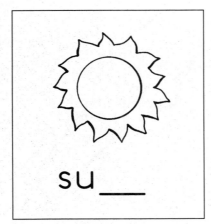

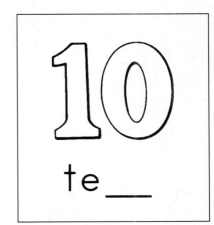

pia___o

su___

we___

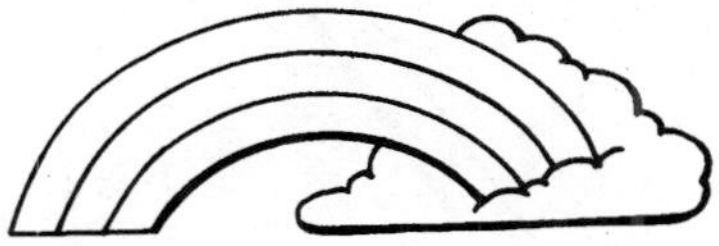

rai___bow

goa___

te___

ma___

mo___

pe___cil

Name ______________________ Date ________________

The Sound of c

Name each picture. Listen to the first sound.
Color the pictures that begin with the **c** sound.

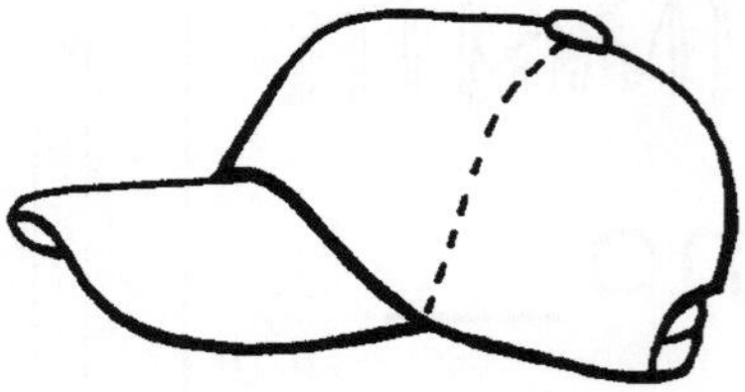

Name ______________________ Date ________________

The Sound of h 

Name each picture. Listen to the first sound. If the name begins with the **h** sound, write **h**.

 ___	 ___	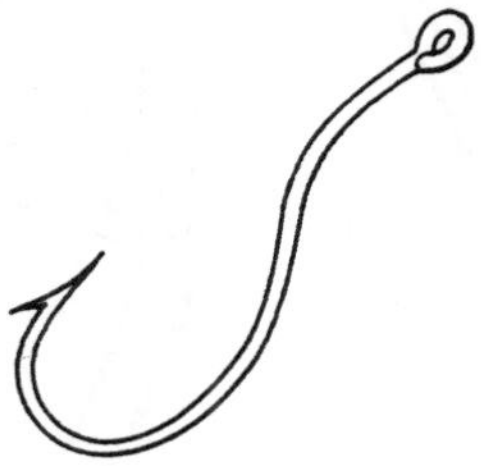 ___	 ___
 ___	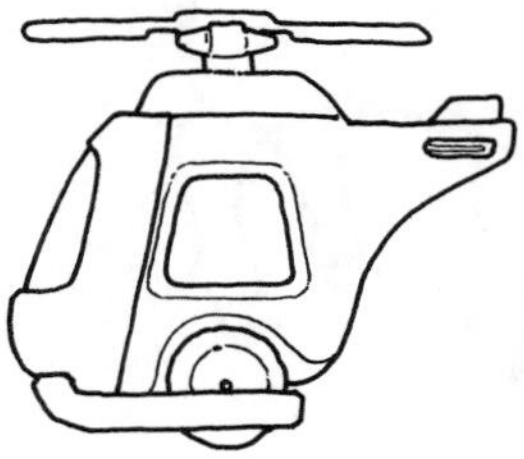 ___	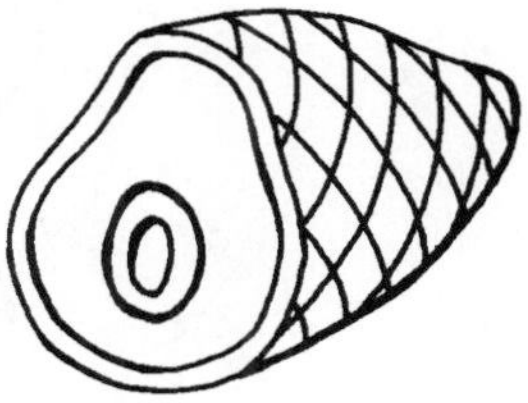 ___	 ___
 ___	 ___	 ___	 ___

Name ______________________ Date ____________________

The Sound of l

Name each picture. Listen to the first sound.
Color the pictures that begin with the **l** sound.

Name ________________________ Date __________________

Missing l

Name each picture. If **l** stands for the missing sound, write **l** on the line.

came___

sea___

sa___ad

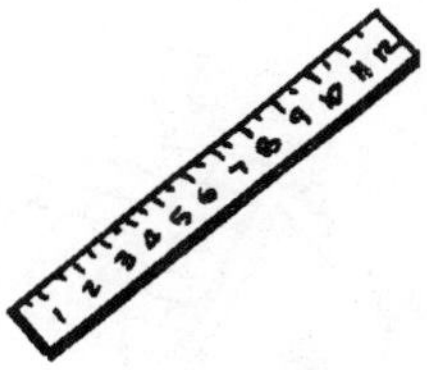

ru___er

pia___o

squirre___

shi___

vio___in

gir___

Name ______________________ Date ________________

The Sound of r 

Name each picture. Listen to the first sound.
If the name begins with the **r** sound, write **r**.

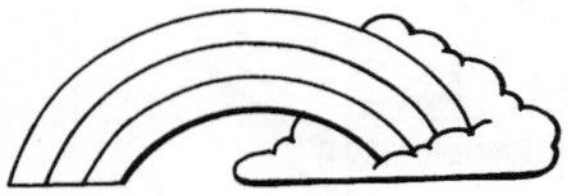 ___	 ___	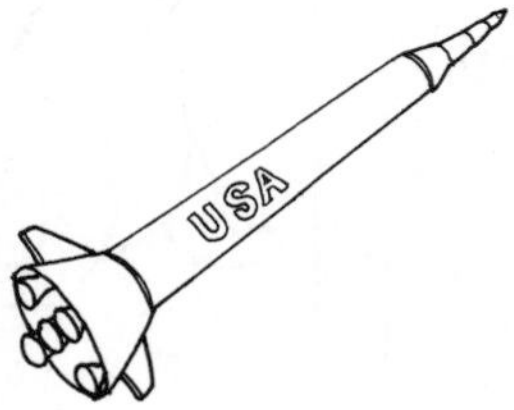 ___	 ___
 ___	 ___	 ___	 ___
 ___	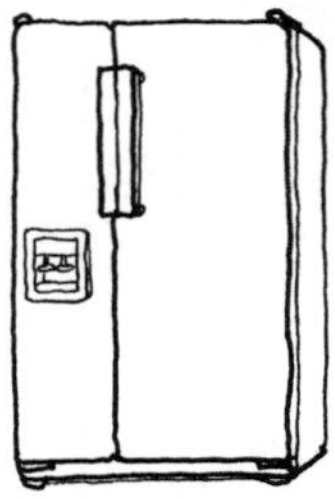 ___	 ___	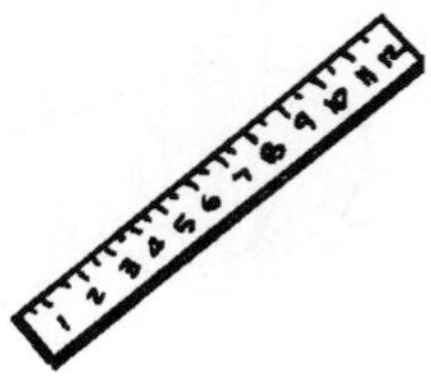 ___

Name ______________________ Date ________________

Missing r

Name each picture. If **r** stands for the missing sound, write **r** on the line.

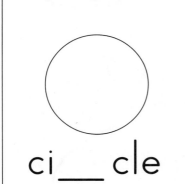

sta___

pen___il

bea___

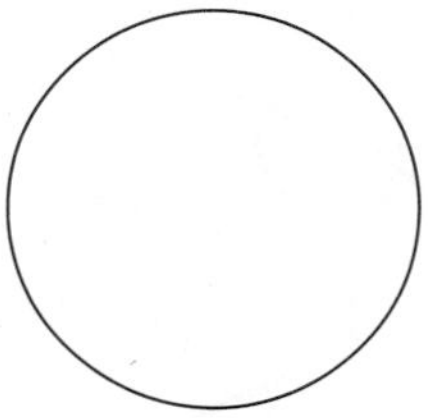

ci___cle

ca___

bi___d

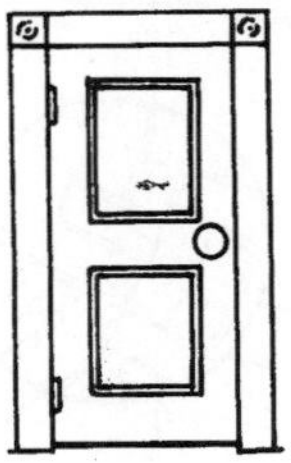

doo___

su___

tu___tle

Name ______________________________ Date ______________________

The Sound of v 

Name each picture. Listen to the first sound.
Color the pictures that begin with the **v** sound.

Name ______________________ Date ________________

Missing v 

Name each picture. If **v** stands for the missing sound, write **v** on the line.

se__ en

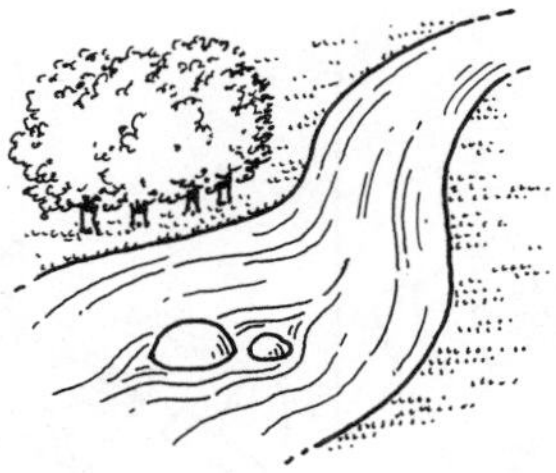

ri__ er

ti__ er

sho__ el

wa__ on

di__ er

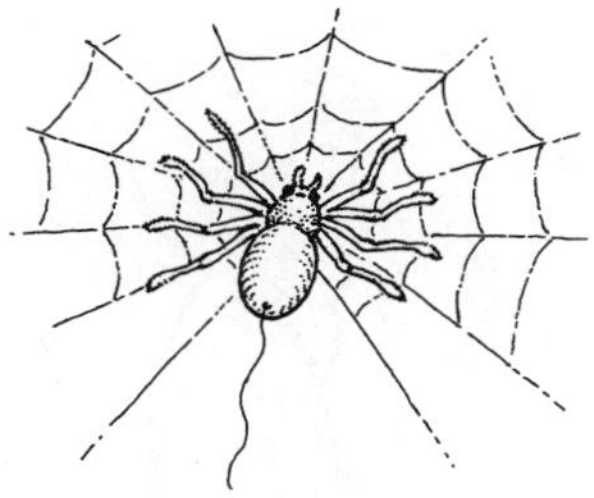

spi__ er

dri__ er

bea__ er

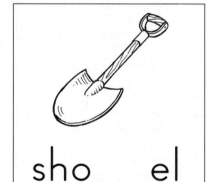

Name ______________________ Date ________________

The Sound of y 

Name each picture. Listen to the first sound.
If the name begins with the **y** sound, write **y**.

___

___

___

___

___

___

___

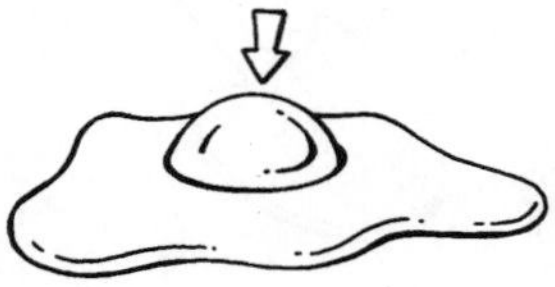
___

___

___

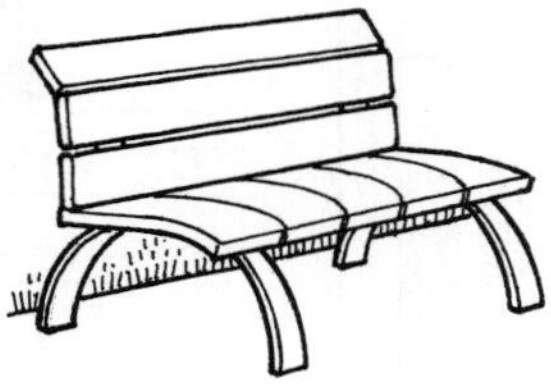
___

___

Name ______________________ Date ______________________

The Sound of z

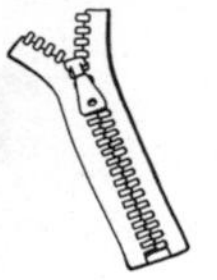

Name each picture. Listen to the first sound.
Color the pictures that begin with the **z** sound.

Name ______________________ Date ________________

The Sound of qu 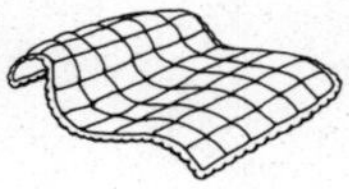

Name each picture. Listen to the first sound.
If the name begins with the **qu** sound, write **qu**.

___

___

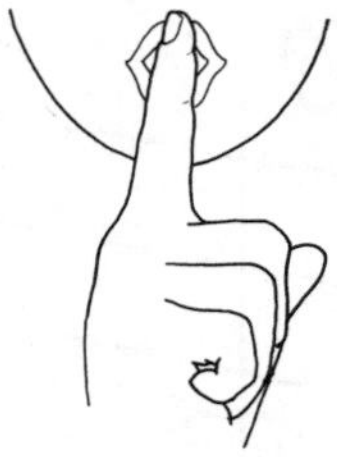

___

___

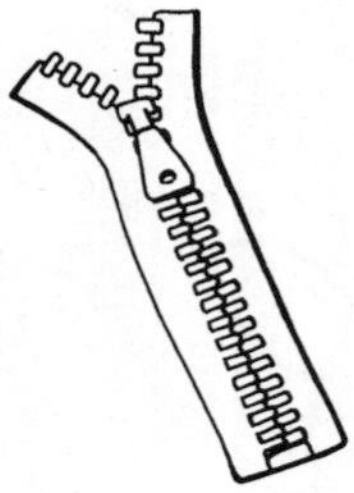

___

___

___

___

___

___

___

___

Name ______________________________ Date ______________________

Missing x 

Name each picture. If the missing sound is the sound you hear at the end of **ax**, write **x** on the line.

si___

o___

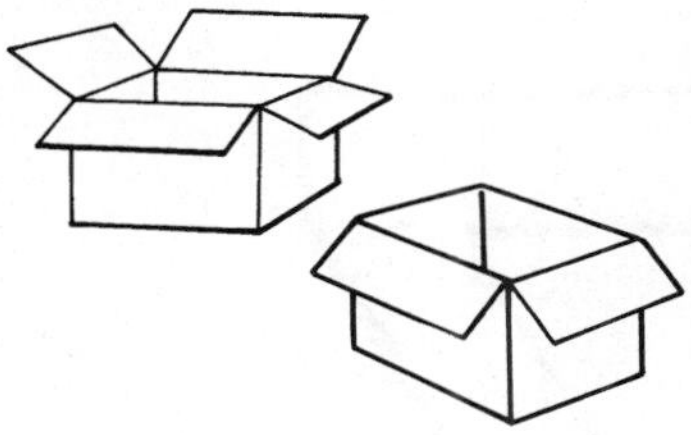

bo___es

wa___on

wa___

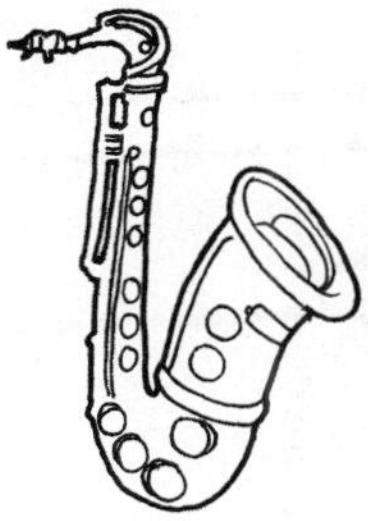

sa___

fo___es

pi___

mi___

Name ______________________________ Date ______________________

Letter Logic

Use the clues to find the word. Fill in the letters that spell the word. Color the picture. Hint: Cross out the pictures as you solve each clue.

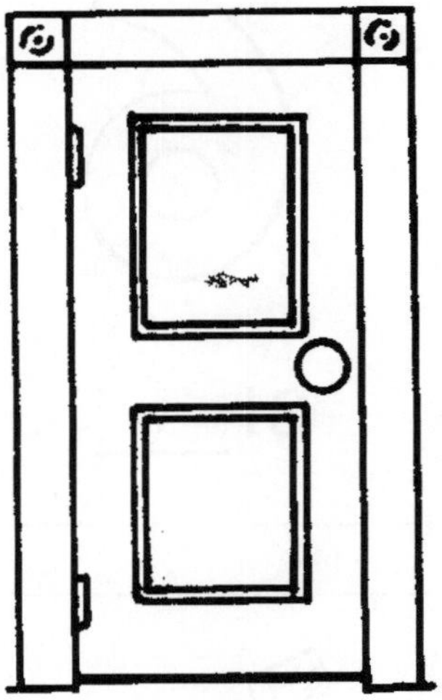
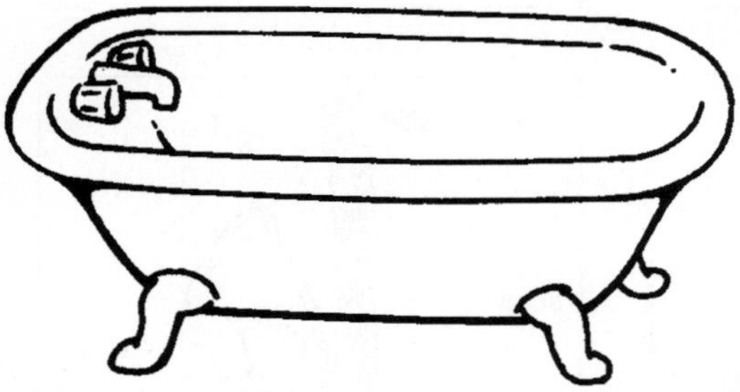

It does not start with **p** or **t**.
It does not end with **x** or **r**.
There is no **v** in it.

It is a ___ a ___ e ___.

Vic has a ____ir____,

a d____g,

and a ____a____.

a ____ea____,

and a ____io____.

What do you think of that?

Do you want a pet?

Draw the pet you want.

Vic's Home Zoo

____

made this book!

Name ______________________________ Date ______________________

Listen for Short a 

Name each picture. Color the pictures that have the short **a** sound.

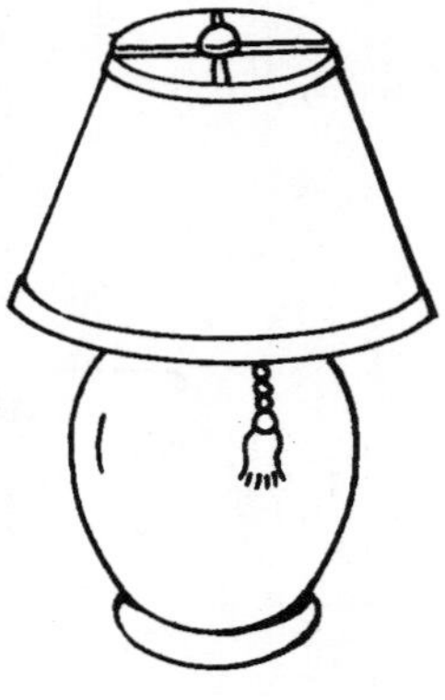

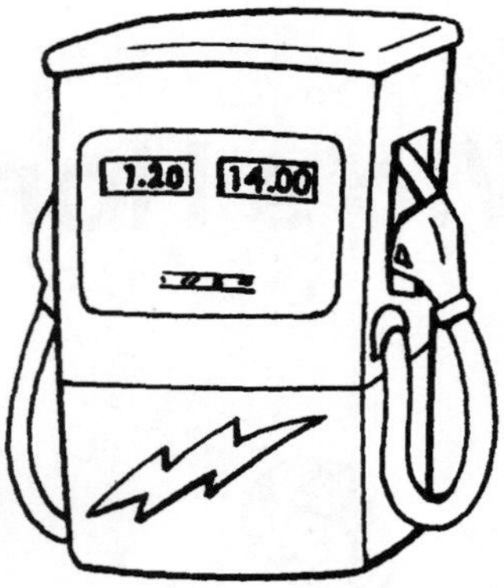

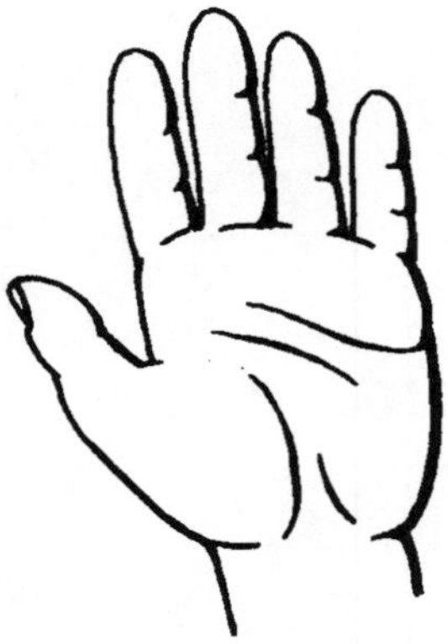

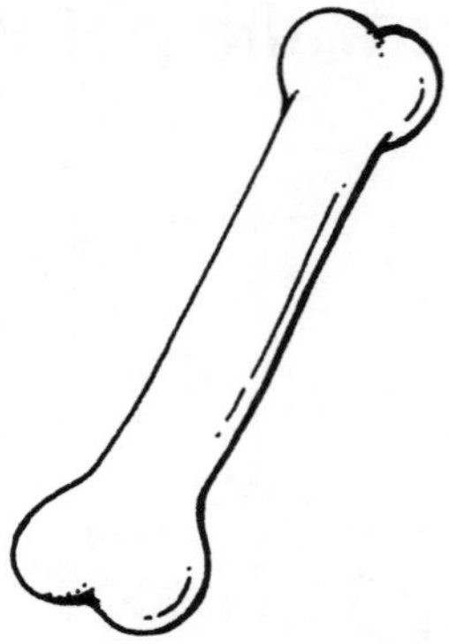

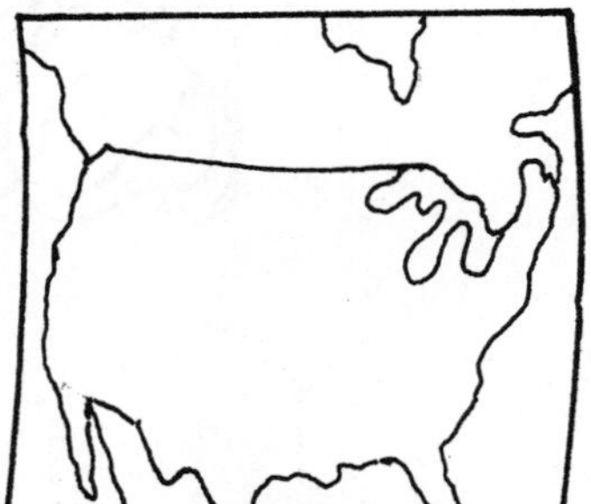

Name ______________________ Date ________________

Hear and Write Short a 

Name each picture. If the name has the short **a** sound, write **a** on the line.

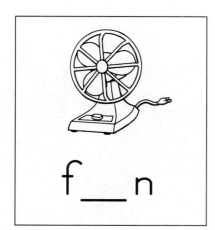

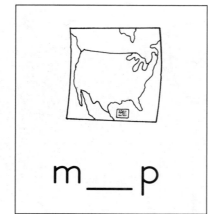

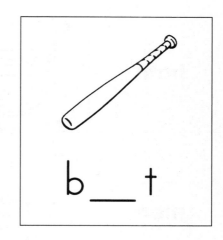

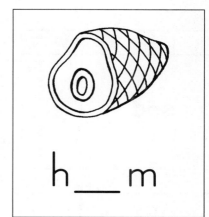

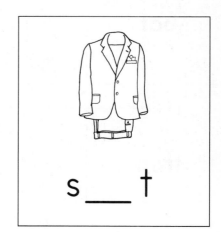

f___n

m___p

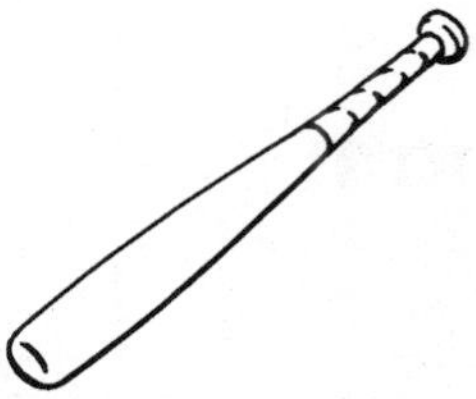

b___t

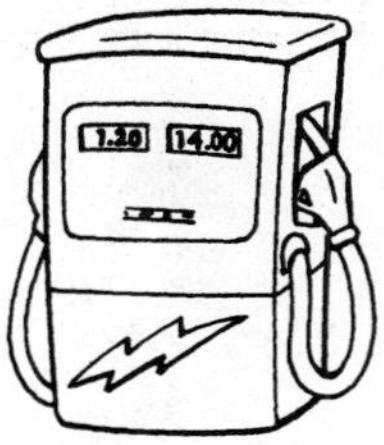

g___s

b___t

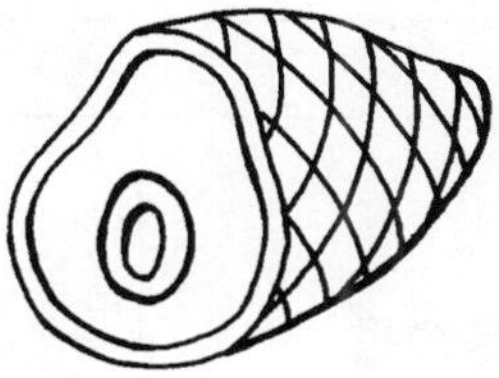

h___m

p___n

h___t

s___t

Name ______________________ Date ________________

Read and Rhyme 

Name each picture. Circle the pictures that rhyme with the word at the beginning of each row.

ham			
man			
sad			
bat			
trap	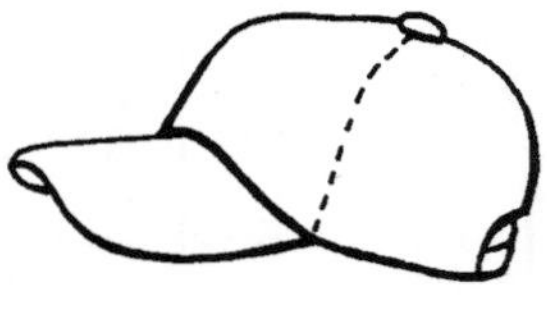		

Name ______________________ Date ______________

Sounds and Sentences

Look at the pictures. Read the sentences. Underline the sentence that tells about each picture.

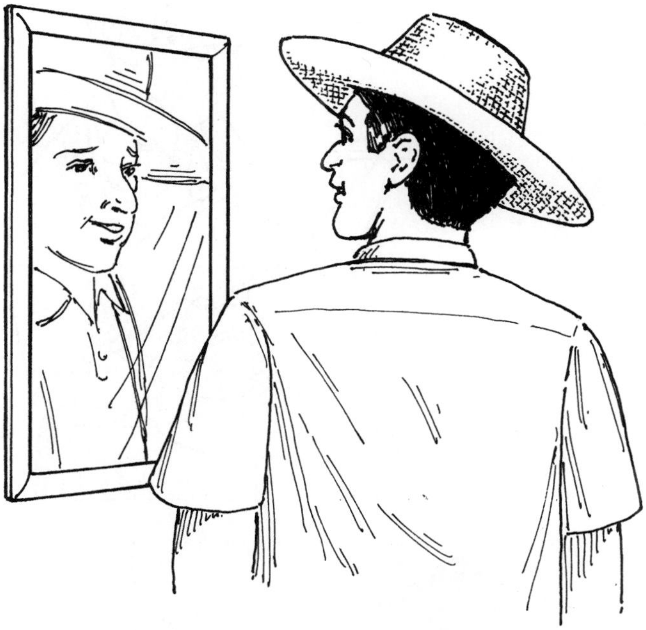

The man has a bag.
Dad has a cup.
Dad has a hat.

The cat is in the bag.
The cat is in the hat.
The bug is in the can.

Name ______________________ Date ______________

Story Time

Read the story. Answer the question. Color the picture.

Ham with Dad

Dad has a pan.
A ham is in the pan.
Not bad!

What is in the pan?

____

Name ______________________ Date ________________

Listen for Short i 

Name each picture. Color the pictures that have the short **i** sound.

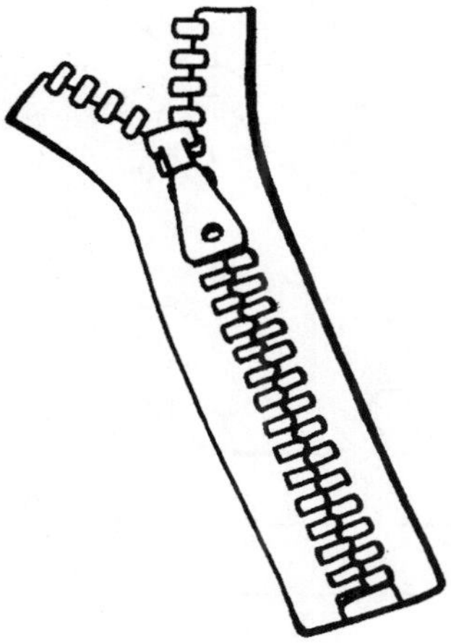

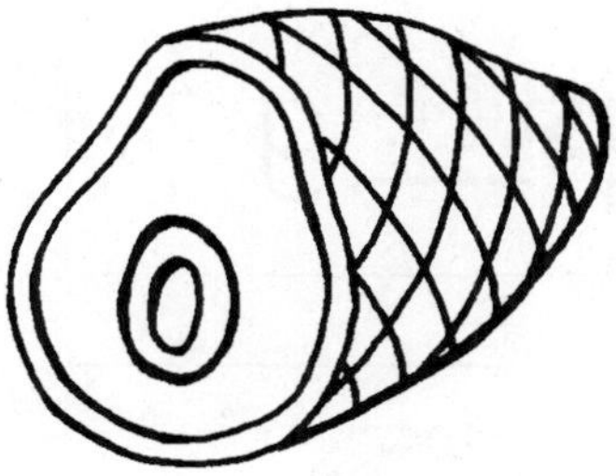

Name ______________________ Date ________________

Hear and Write Short i

Name each picture. If the name has the short **i** sound, write **i** on the line.

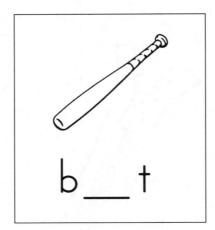

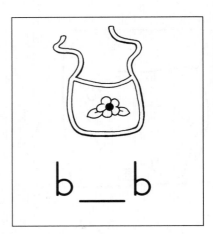

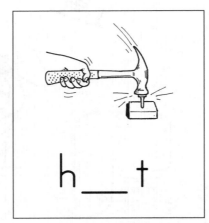

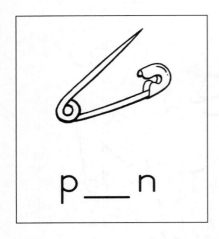

m ___ x

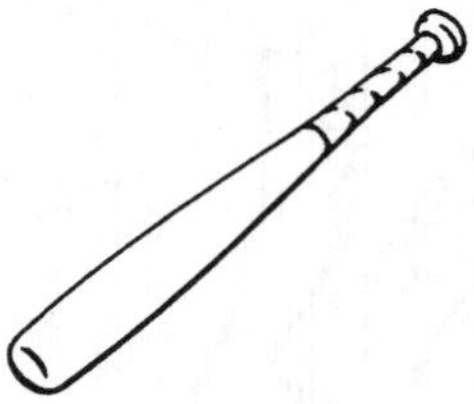

b ___ t

b ___ b

p ___ n

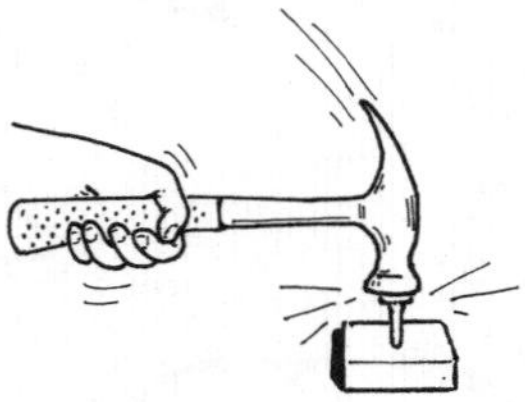

h ___ t

p ___ g

p ___ n

s ___ x

w ___ g

Name ______________________________ Date ______________________

Read and Rhyme

Name each picture. Circle the pictures that rhyme with the word at the beginning of each row.

win			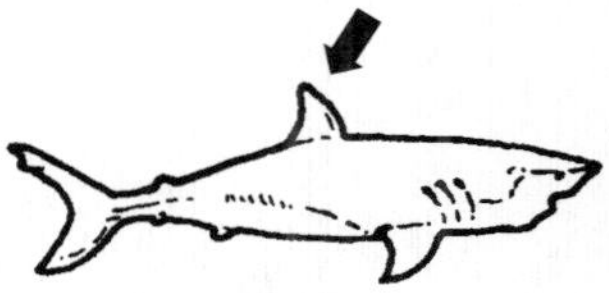
dip		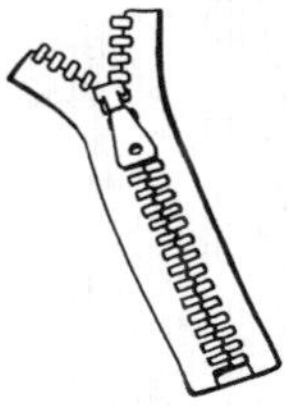	
will			
wig	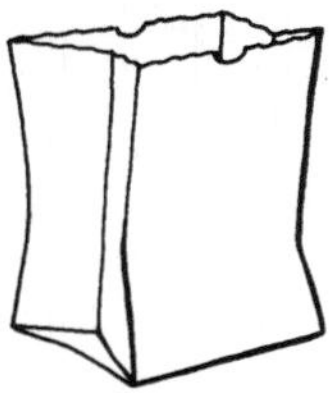		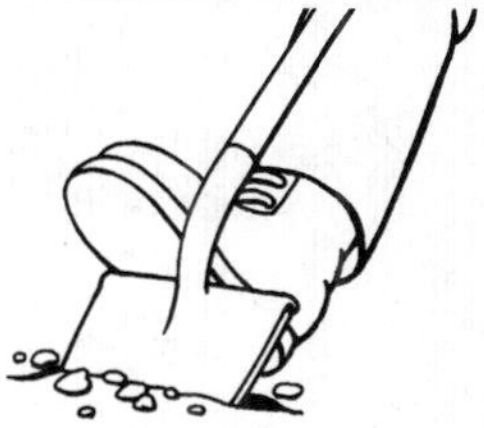
sit	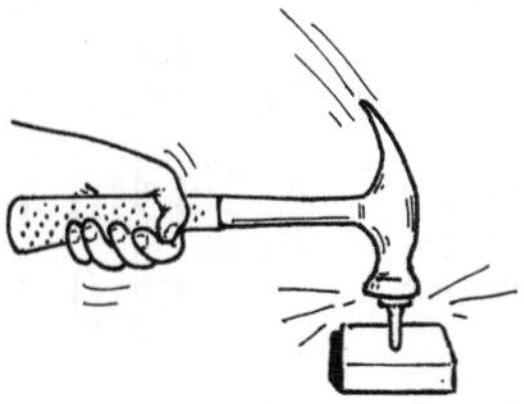		

Name________________________ Date__________________

Sounds and Sentences

Look at the pictures. Read the sentences. Underline the sentence that tells about each picture.

Kim has a big hat.
Kim can dig a big pit.
Did Kim sit on a pin?

Bill is sick.
Bill has a pig.
Bill has six cats.

Name ______________________ Date ______________

Story Time

Read the story. Answer the question. Color the picture.

Will Liz Win?

Liz is at bat.
Can Liz hit the ball?
Liz hits it!
Liz wins.

How did Liz win?

____

____

Name ______________________ Date ______________

Listen for Short o 

Name each picture. Color the pictures that have the short **o** sound.

Name ______________________________ Date ______________________

Hear and Write Short o

Name each picture. If the name has the short **o** sound, write **o** on the line.

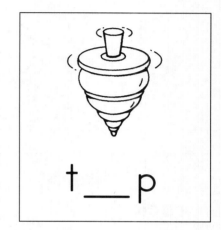

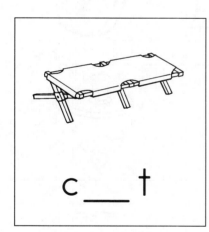

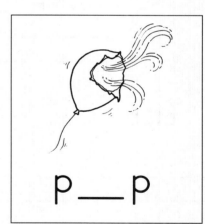

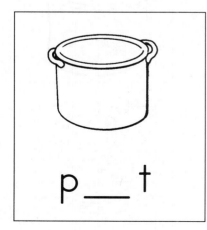

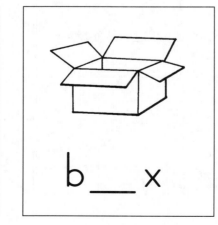

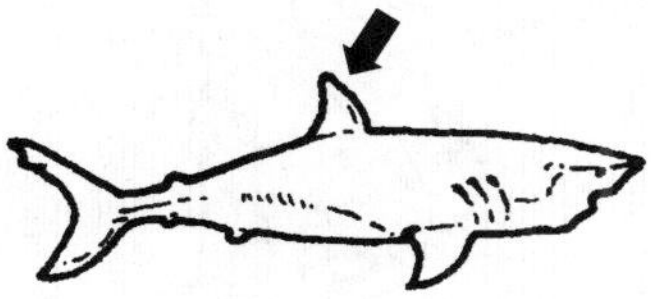

f___n

f___x

t___p

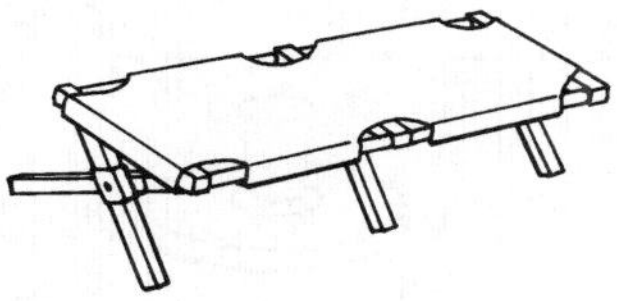

c___t

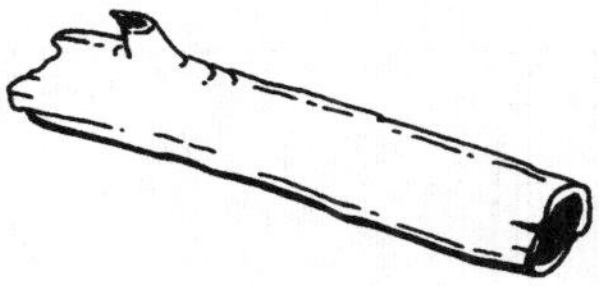

l___g

p___p

p___t

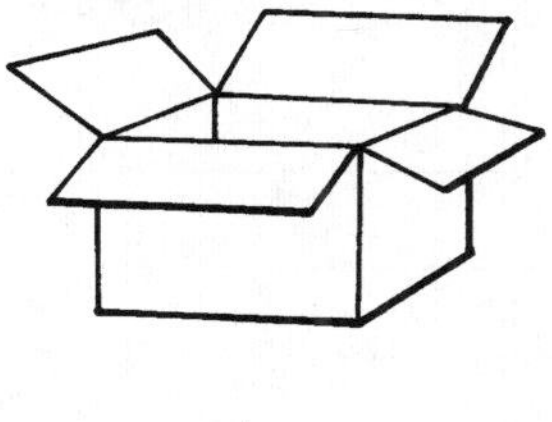

b___x

f___n

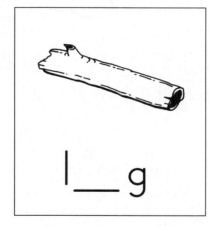

Name ______________________________ Date ______________________

Read and Rhyme

Name each picture. Circle the pictures that rhyme with the word at the beginning of each row.

log			
rock			
stop			
got		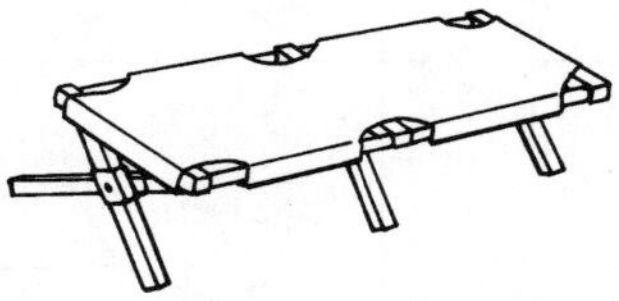	
ox		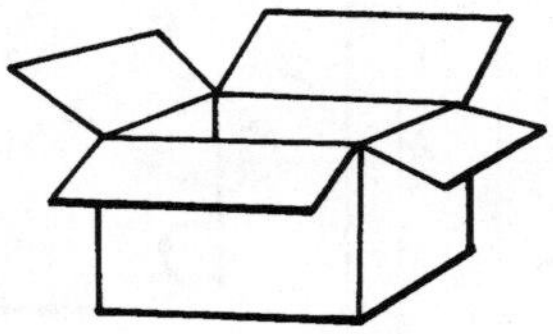	

Name ______________________ Date ______________

Sounds and Sentences

Look at the pictures. Read the sentences. Underline the sentence that tells about each picture.

The fox hops in the box.
The ox stops at the log.
The fox jogs to the log.

The hat is in the box.
The top is not in the box.
The box is on the cot.

Name____________________________ Date____________________

Story Time

Read the story. Answer the question. Color the picture.

A Box That Hops

A frog spots Roz.
Roz spots a box.
The box hops.

What is in the box?

____

____

Name_______________________________ Date________________________

Listen for Short u 

Name each picture. Color the pictures that have the short **u** sound.

Name ____________________ Date ____________________

Hear and Write Short u 

Name each picture. If the name has the short **u** sound, write **u** on the line.

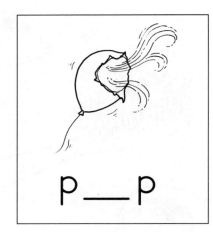

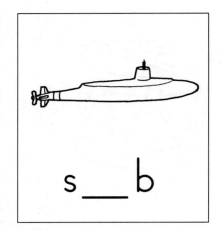

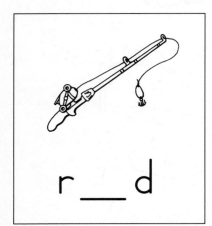

c___p

p___p

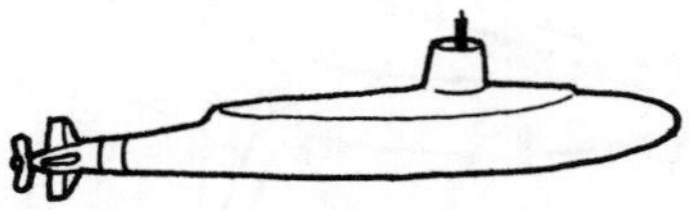

s___b

p___p

s___n

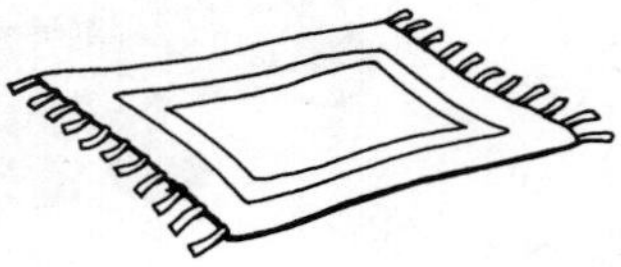

r___g

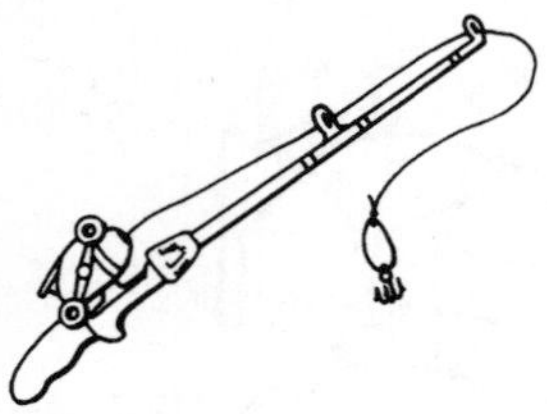

r___d

r___n

b___g

Name____________________________ Date____________________

Read and Rhyme

Name each picture. Circle the pictures that rhyme with the word at the beginning of each row.

fun			
rug		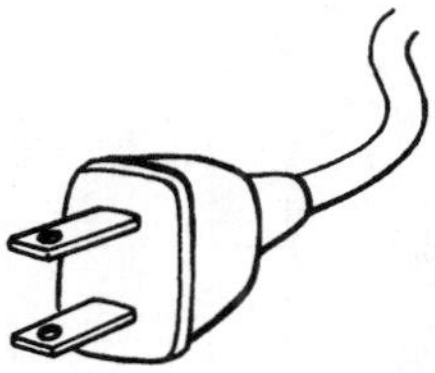	
hut	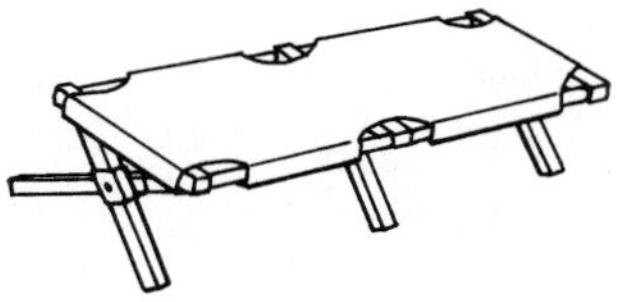		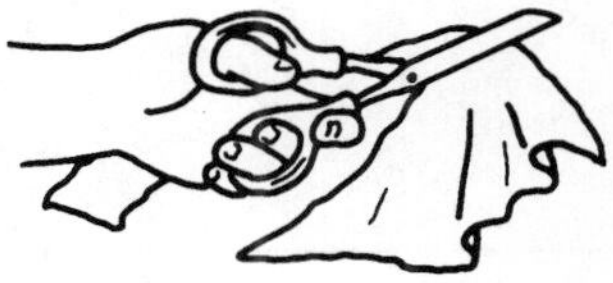
plum		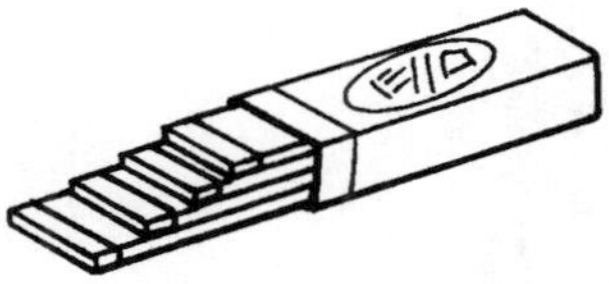	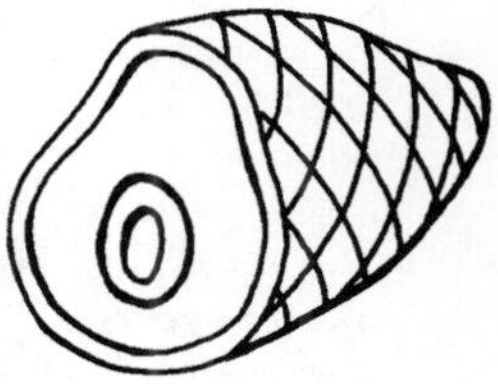
sub			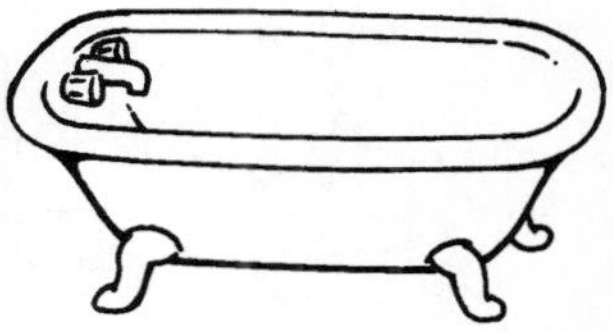

Name ______________________ Date ______________________

Sounds and Sentences

Look at the pictures. Read the sentences. Underline the sentence that tells about each picture.

The cub is in the bus.
The cub jumps at the bug.
The cub runs in the sun.

The pup is in the tub.
The pup tugs on the rug.
The pup is under the tub.

Name ______________________ Date ________________

Story Time

Read the story. Answer the question. Color the picture.

Stuck in Gum

Bob drops his gum.
Bob will not pick it up.
Bob runs in the gum.
Now Bob is stuck.

Why is Bob stuck?

____

____

____

Name______________________ Date________________

Listen for Short e 

Name each picture. Color the pictures that have the short **e** sound.

Name ______________________ Date ________________

Hear and Write Short e 

Name each picture. If the name has the short **e** sound, write **e** on the line.

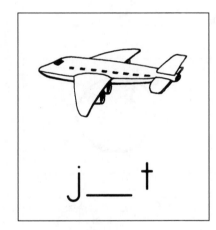

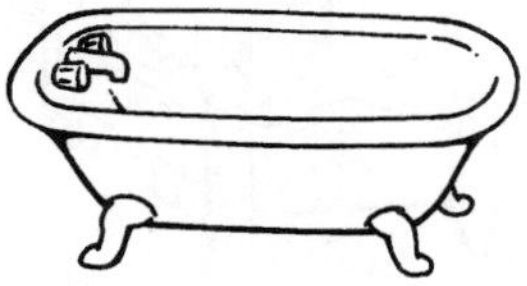 t ___ b	 m ___ n	 n ___ t
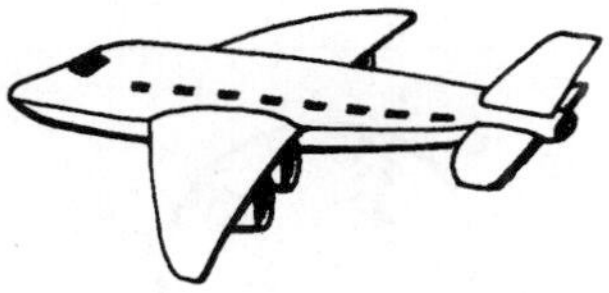 j ___ t	 w ___ b	 t ___ n
 p ___ n	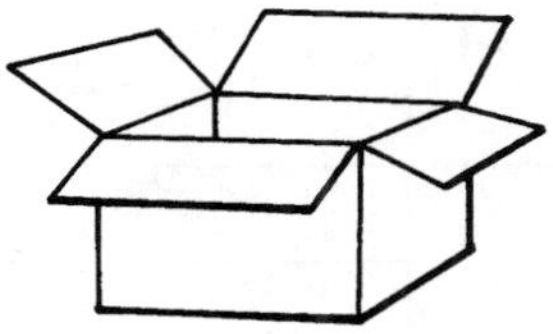 b ___ x	 b ___ d

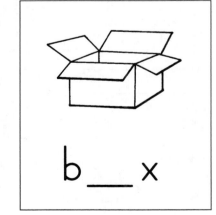

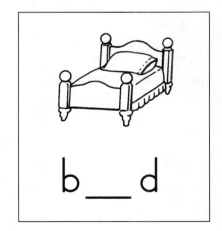

Name ______________________________ Date ____________________

Read and Rhyme

Name each picture. Circle the pictures that rhyme with the word at the beginning of each row.

sled			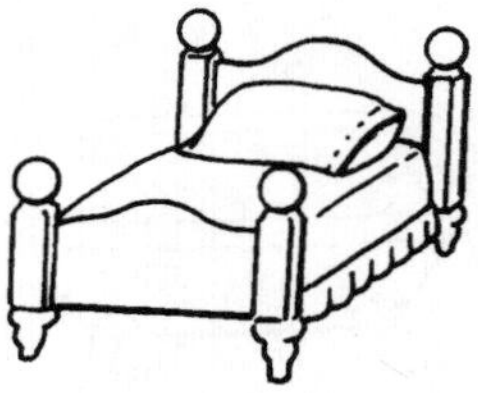
den			
yell		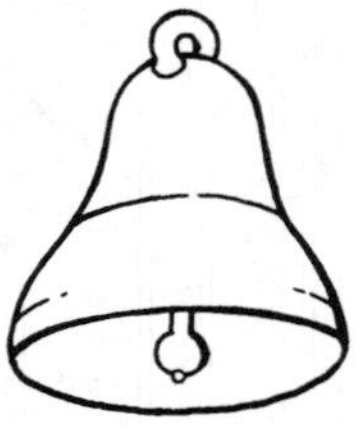	
pet			
peg		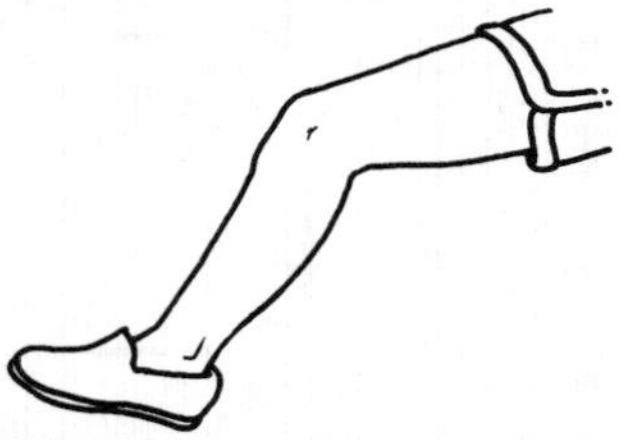	

Name ______________________ Date ________________

Sounds and Sentences 

Look at the pictures. Read the sentences. Underline the sentence that tells about each picture.

The pet is wet.
The pet is in a net.
The vet helps the pet.

Ken is in the den.
Ken is all wet.
Ken has a pen.

Name ______________________ Date ________________

Story Time

Read the story. Answer the question. Color the picture.

Peg and Jen

Jen is in the pen.
Jen is a sick hen.
Peg gets in the pen with Jen.
Peg will help Jen get well.

What will Peg do for Jen?

____

- -

____

The Best Pet of All

____

made this book!

Jeb can sit up and beg.

Jeb can get a ball.

Jeb can ring a bell.

Jeb is the best.

What else can Jeb do?

Draw a new trick for Jeb.

Name________________________ Date____________________

Listen for Long a

Name each picture. Color the pictures that have the long **a** sound.

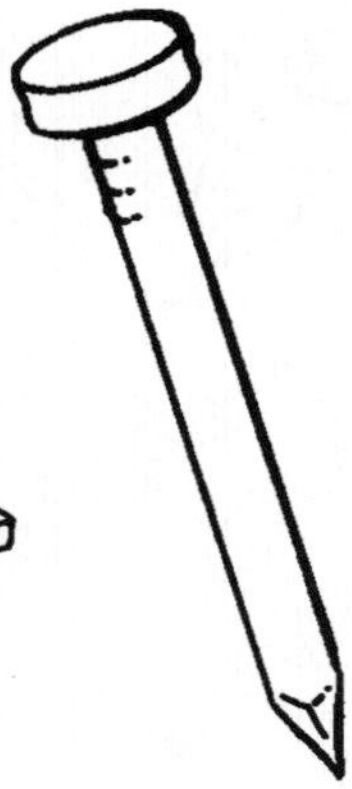
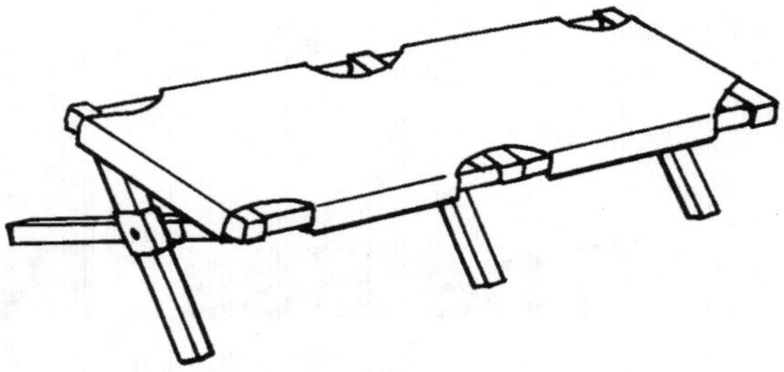

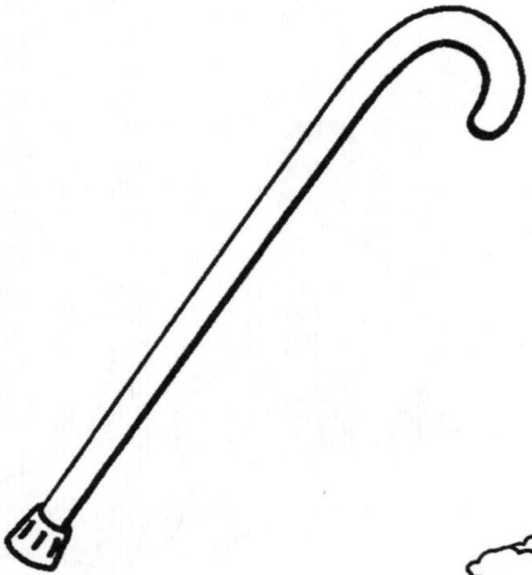

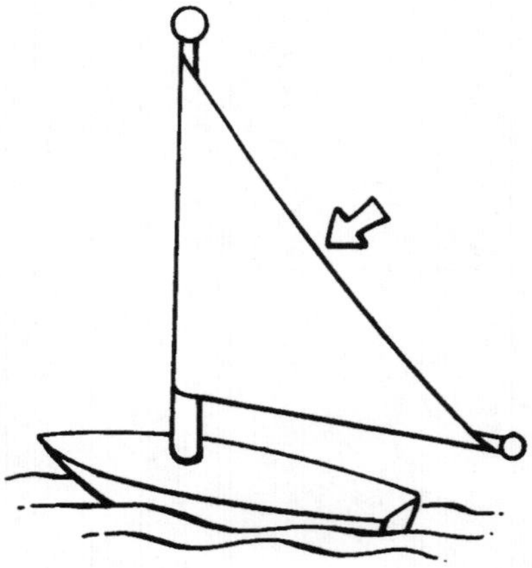

Name ______________________ Date ________________

Hear and Write Long a

The letters **a__e** can stand for the long **a** sound. Name each picture. If the name has the long **a** sound, write **a** and **e** on the lines.

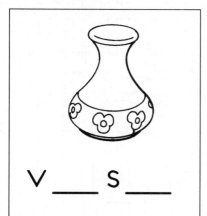

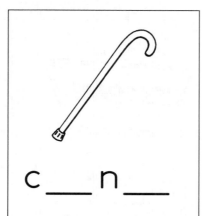

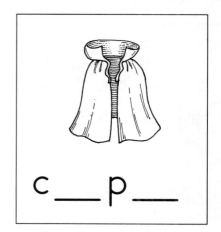

v___ s___

c___ n___

c___ n___

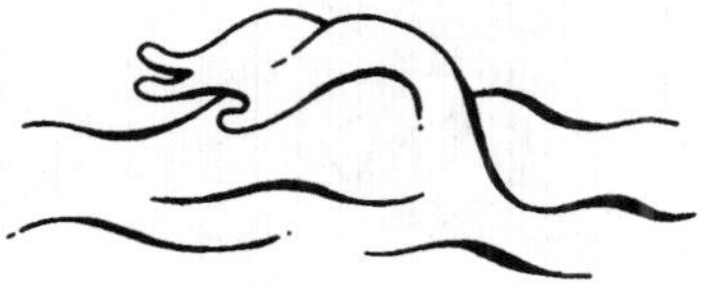

w___ v___

w___ b___

l___ k___

n___ t___

g___ m___

c___ p___

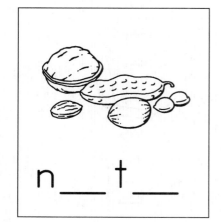

Name ____________________ Date ____________________

Hear and Write Long a

The letters **ai** can stand for the long **a** sound. Name each picture. If the name has the long **a** sound, write **ai** on the line.

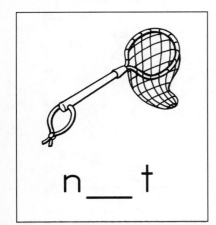

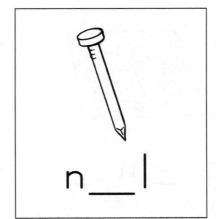

t ___ l

m ___ t

m ___ l

w ___ t

r ___ l

w ___ t

n ___ t

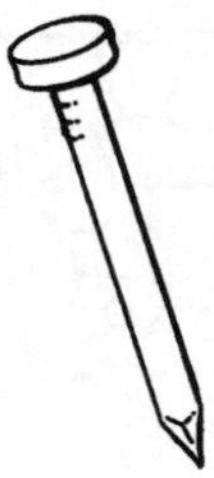

n ___ l

p ___ l

Name ____________________ Date ____________________

Hear and Write Long a 

The letters **ay** can stand for the long **a** sound. Name each picture. If the name has the long **a** sound, write **ay** on the line.

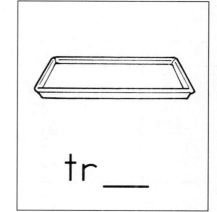

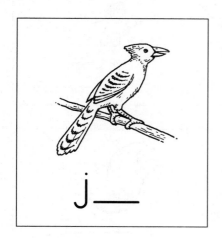

j___

c___

pl___

h___

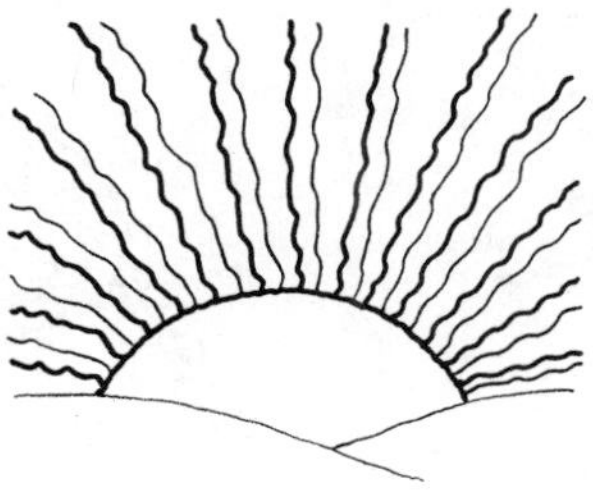

r___

r___

d___

h___

tr___

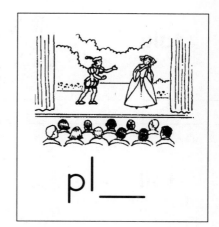

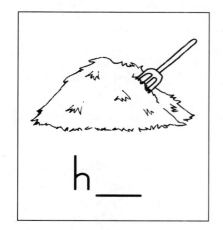

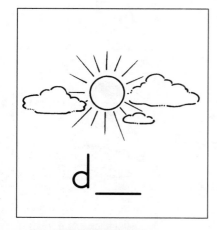

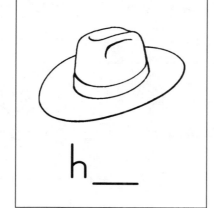

Name ______________________ Date ________________

Read and Rhyme

Name each picture. Circle the pictures that rhyme with the word at the beginning of each row.

take	  
rail	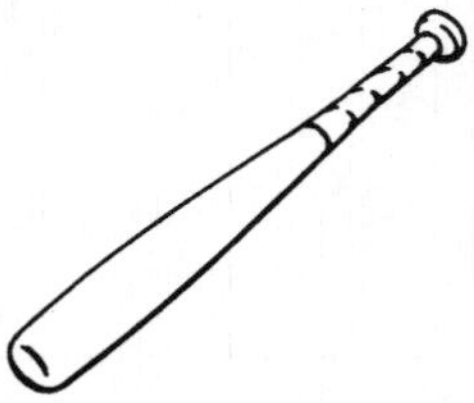 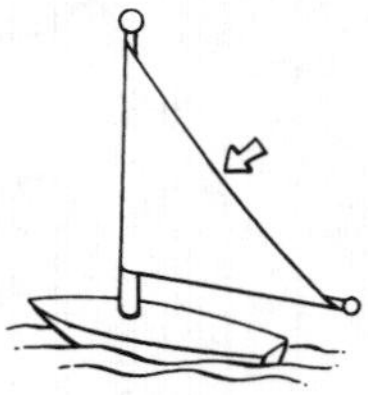 
stay	  
ape	 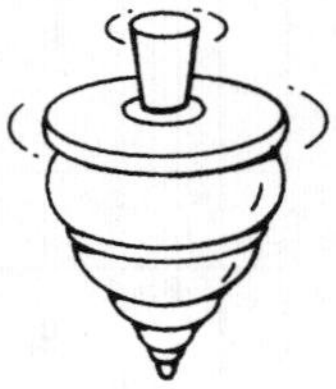 
play	  

Name ____________________ Date ____________________

Sounds and Sentences

Circle the word with the long **a** sound that completes the sentence. Write it on the line.

1. Do you want a ____________________?

bat
cake
cat

2. I ____________________ it.

mad
pail
made

3. You will have to ____________________.

wait
way
wet

4. You can ____________________ Dave.

pay
pan
pail

5. Here is a ____________________.

play
plate
pen

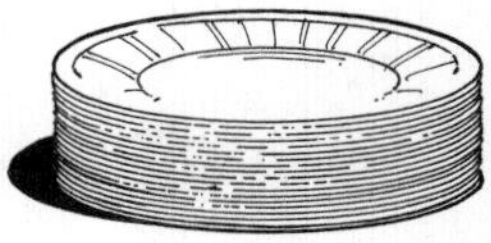

6. Now you can ____________________ it.

tack
tip
take

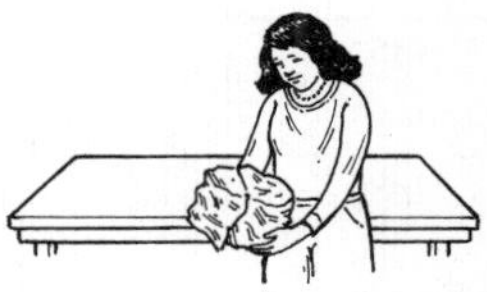

Name ______________________ Date ________________

Story Time

Read the story. Answer the question. Color the picture.

The Lake

The lake is fun.
We use a sand pail.
We may sail, too.
If it rains, we play games.

What can you do at the lake?

____

____

Name ______________________ Date ________________

Listen for Long i 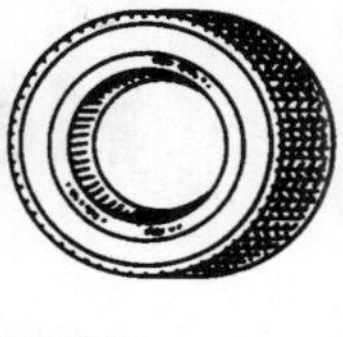

Name each picture. Color the pictures that have the long **i** sound.

Name ______________________ Date ________________

Hear and Write Long i 

The letters **i__e** can stand for the long **i** sound. Name each picture. If the name has the long **i** sound, write **i** and **e** on the lines.

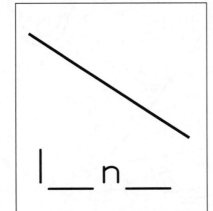

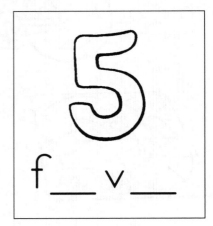

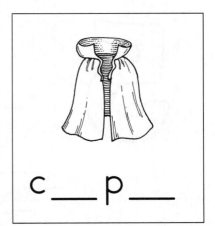

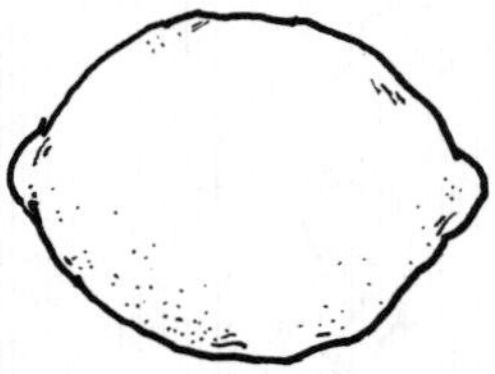

l__m__

p__n__

g__m__

l__k__

m__c__

f__v__

d__m__

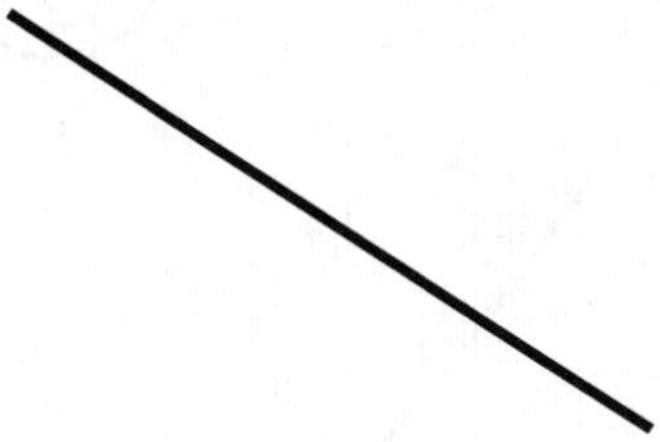

l__n__

c__p__

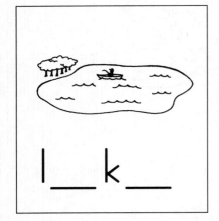

Name ______________________ Date ________________

Read and Rhyme

Name each picture. Circle the pictures that rhyme with the word at the beginning of each row.

fine	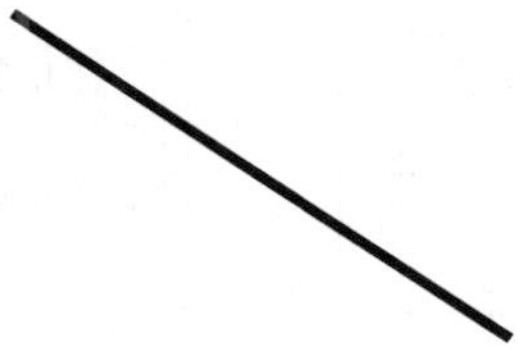		
time		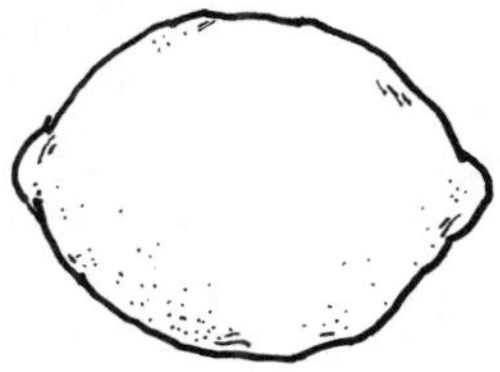	
nice			
hive			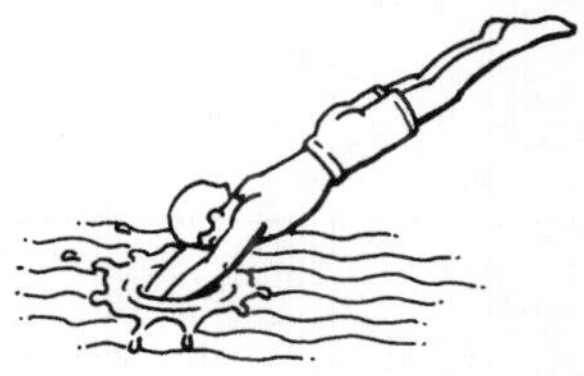
mine			

Name ______________________ Date ______________________

Sounds and Sentences

Circle the word with the long **i** sound that completes the sentence. Write it on the line.

1. Mike is on his ______________.

bet
bake
bike

2. It is a ______________ day to ride.

fine
fin
fan

3. Mike fills up his ______________.

tame
tire
tip

4. He rides by a ______________ tree.

pain
pan
pine

5. It is ______________ to rest.

time
tea
tail

6. Then Mike will fly his ______________.

kite
kit
cake

Name ______________________________ Date ______________________

Story Time

Read the story. Answer the question. Color the picture.

Spike Hides

Spike likes to hide.
The pup hides by the pines.
Dinah finds Spike.
"I see you, Spike!" yells Dinah.
Spike likes Dinah.
Spike runs to Dinah.

What game does Spike like to play?

____

____

Name ______________________ Date ________________

Listen for Long o

Name each picture. Color the pictures that have the long **o** sound.

Name ______________________ Date ________________

Hear and Write Long o 

The letters **o__e** can stand for the long **o** sound. Name each picture. If the name has the long **o** sound, write **o** and **e** on the lines.

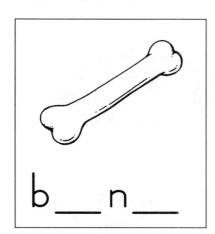

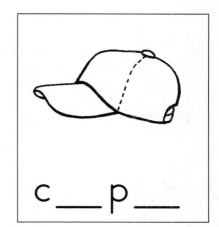

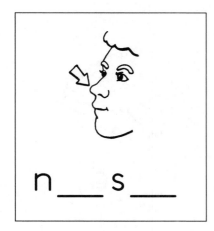

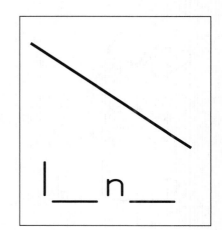

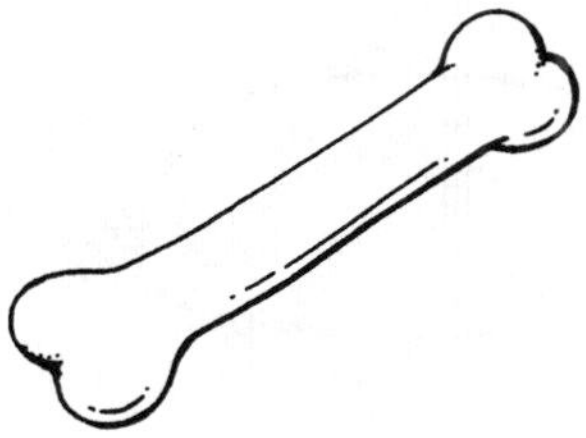

b___ n___

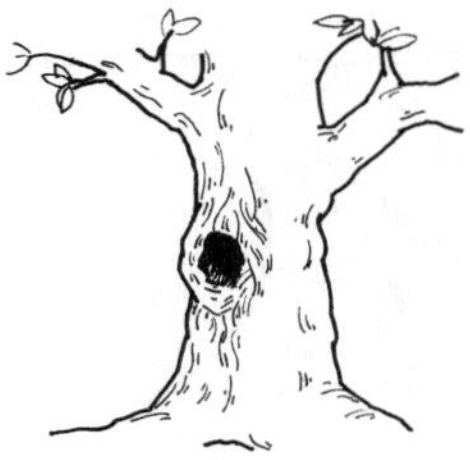

h___ l___

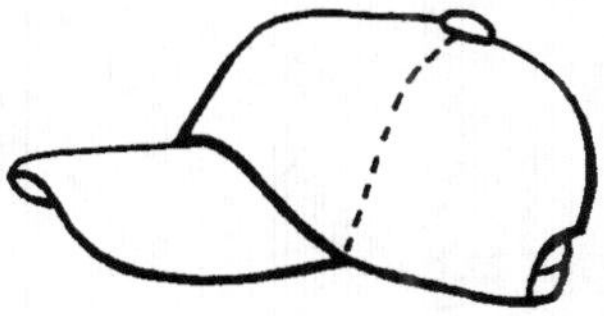

c___ p___

n___ s___

n___ t___

n___ t___

r___ p___

h___ s___

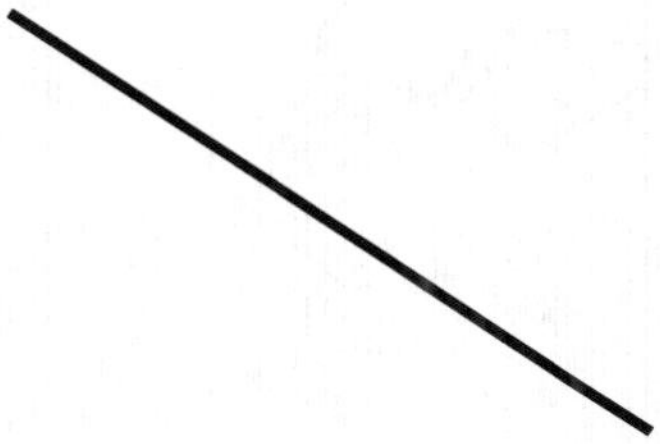

l___ n___

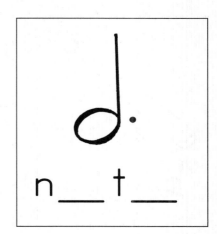

Name________________________ Date__________________

Hear and Write Long o

The letters **oa** can stand for the long **o** sound. Name each picture. If the name has the long **o** sound, write **oa** on the line.

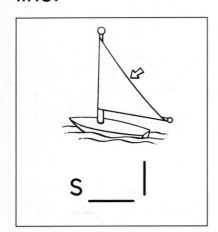

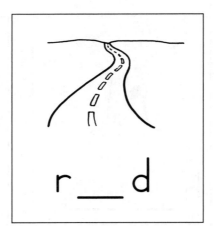

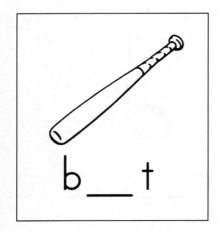

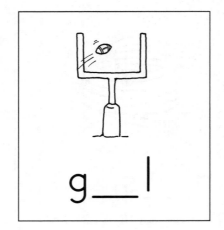

s___l

r___d

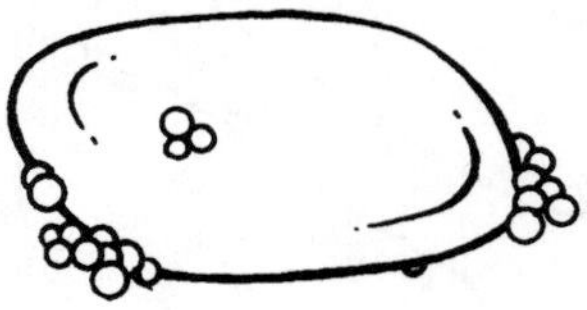

s___p

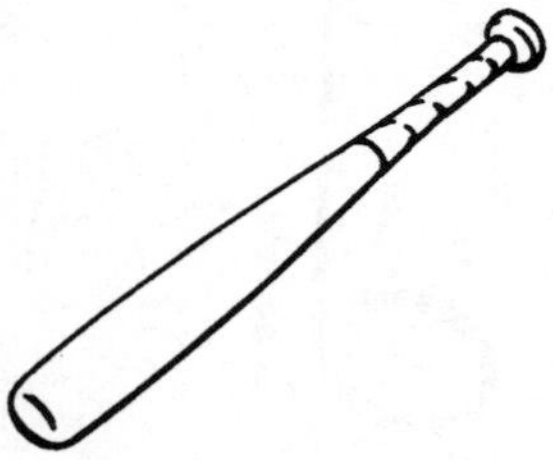

b___t

b___t

t___d

c___l

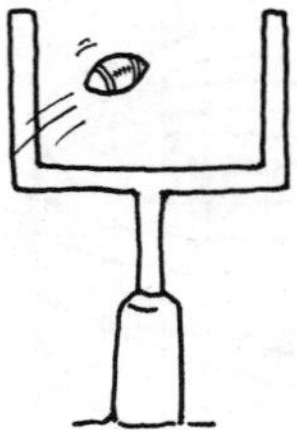

g___l

m___l

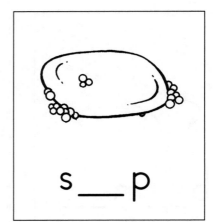

Name ______________________ Date ________________

Read and Rhyme

Name each picture. Circle the pictures that rhyme with the word at the beginning of each row.

bone		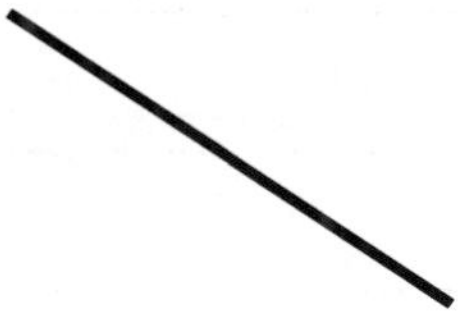	
coat		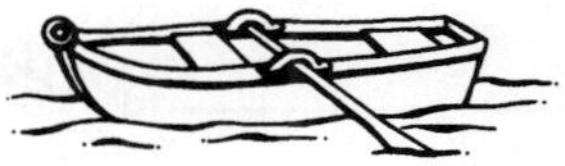	
nose			
load		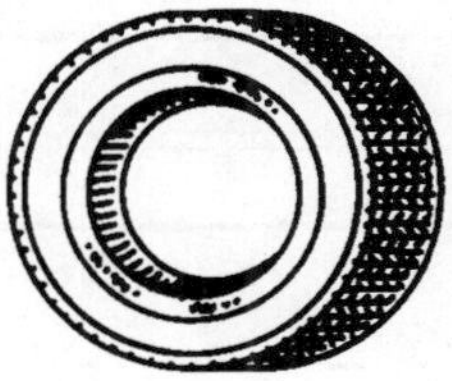	
coal		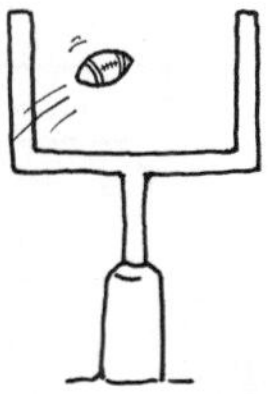	

Name ______________________ Date ________________

Sounds and Sentences

Circle the word with the long **o** sound that completes the sentence. Write it on the line.

1. What is in the ______________?

hill
hole
hall

2. A ______________ pokes up.

nose
nice
nail

3. It is a ______________.

ten
toad
tide

4. Joan ______________ it up.

wig
woke
wail

5. Joan runs ______________.

him
hive
home

6. The toad hops to the ______________.

boat
bite
bat

Name ______________________________ Date ______________________

Story Time

Read the story. Answer the question. Color the picture.

A Hole for a Bone

Mo has a bone.
Mo digs a big hole.
Mo digs up the rose.
"Oh, no!" yells Pop.
"The hole is for the rose."

Why did the dog dig a hole?

____

____

Name ______________________________ Date ______________________

Listen for Long u

Name each picture. Color the pictures that have the long **u** sound.

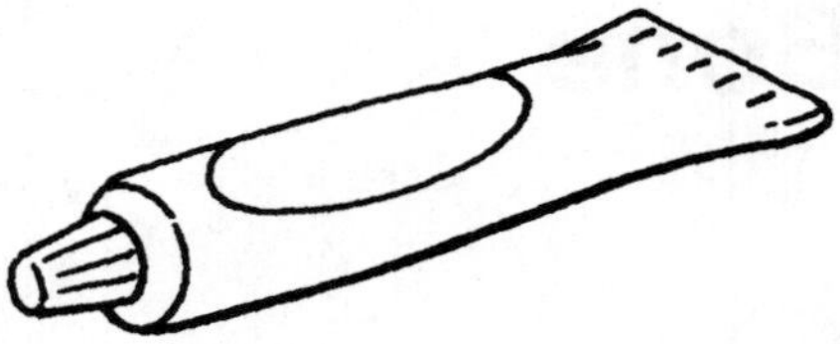

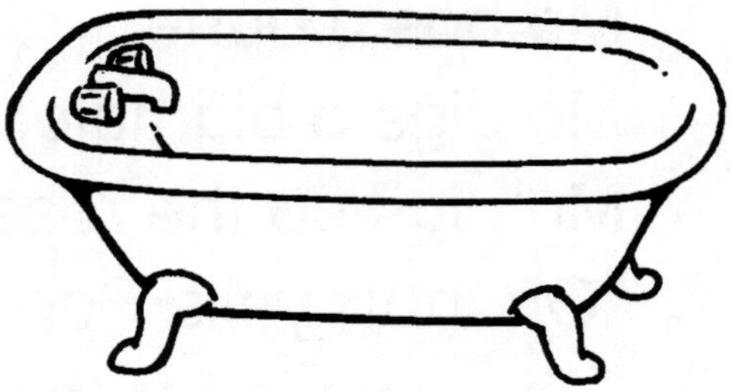

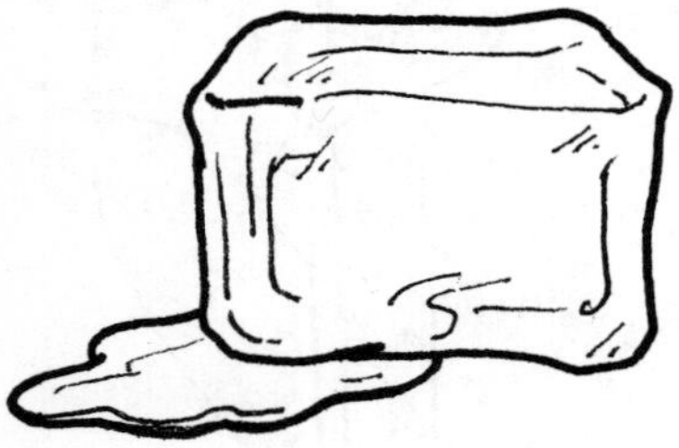

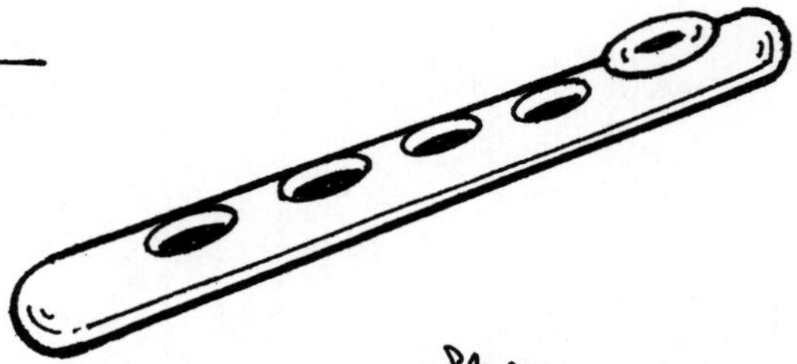

Name ________________________ Date ________________

Hear and Write Long u

The letters **u__e** can stand for the long **u** sound. Name each picture. If the name has the long **u** sound, write **u** and **e** on the lines.

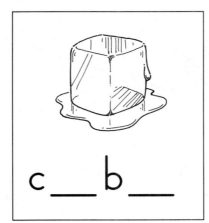

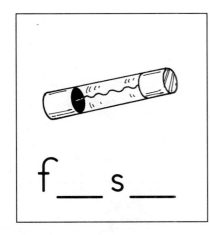

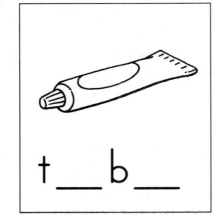

c__ b__

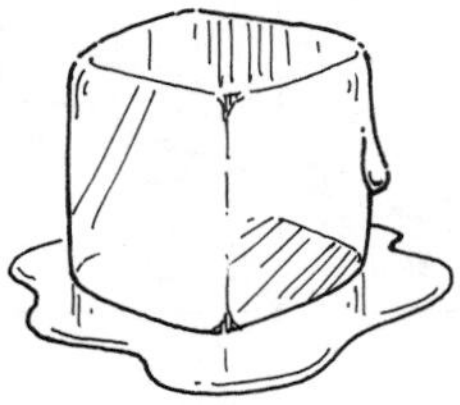

c__ b__

d__ n__

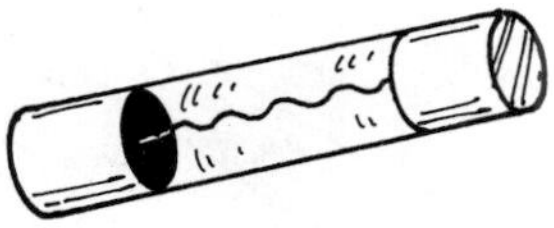

f__ s__

J__ n__

f__ n__

t__ n__

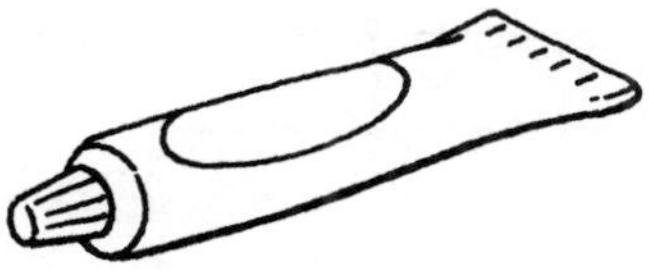

t__ b__

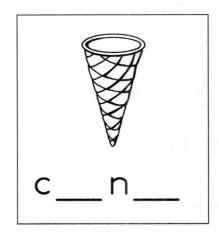

c__ n__

Name ______________________ Date ________________

Read and Rhyme

Name each picture. Circle the pictures that rhyme with the word at the beginning of each row.

cube	 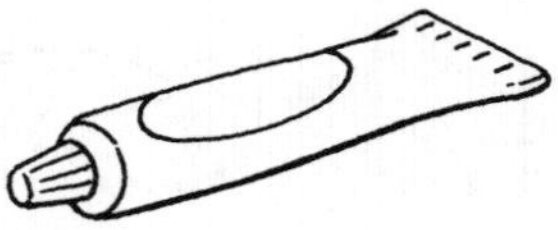 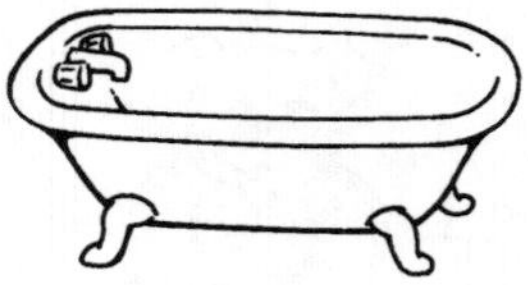
use	  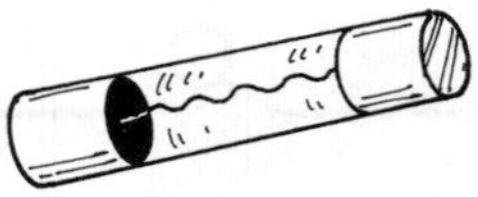
June	  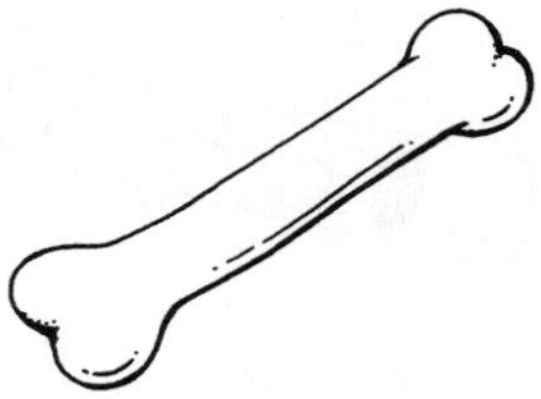
cute	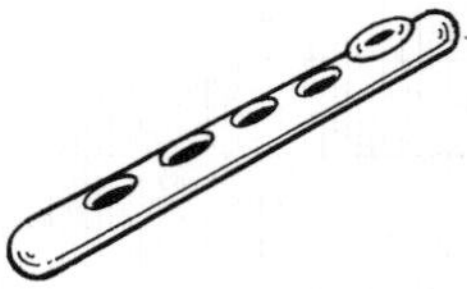 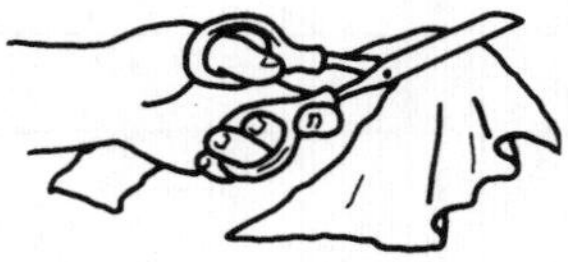 
blue	  

Name ______________________ Date ________________

Sounds and Sentences

Circle the word with the long **u** sound that completes the sentence. Write it on the line.

1. Luke is a ______________.	mule mug mile	
2. Rick can ride ______________.	Like Lake Luke	
3. Rick rides to the ______________.	dune dad den	
4. Luke eats an ice ______________.	cube cane cub	
5. Rick takes a ______________ ride.	tube tub top	
6. What a ______________ mule!	cat cut cute	

Name ______________________________ Date ______________________

Story Time

Read the story. Answer the question. Color the picture.

A Nice Tune

June has a flute.
She can use it to play a tune.
Jules likes the tune.
He hands June a huge rose.

Why did June get a rose?

____

____

____

Name ______________________________ Date ____________________

Listen for Long e 

Name each picture. Color the pictures that have the long **e** sound.

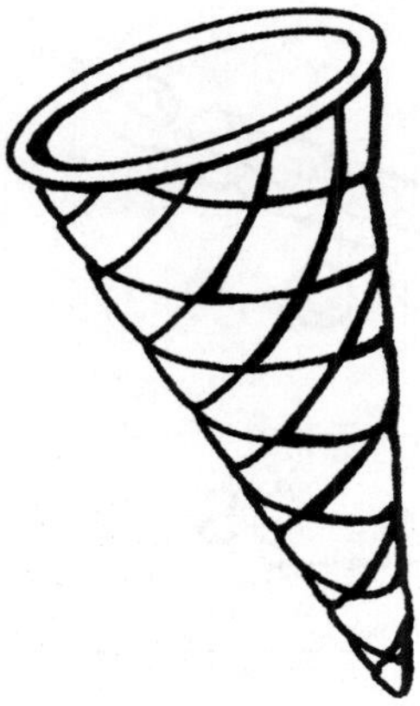

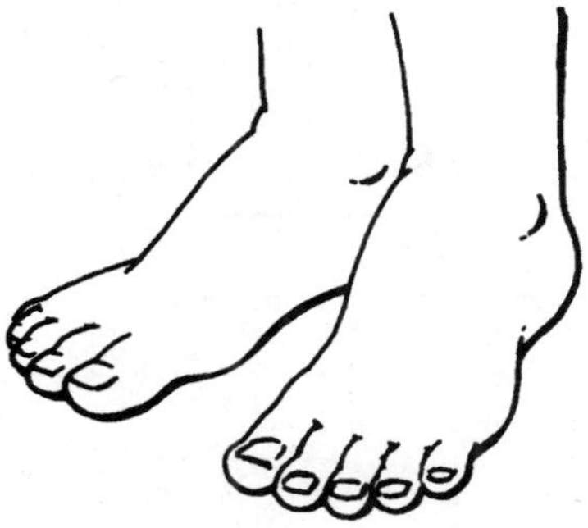

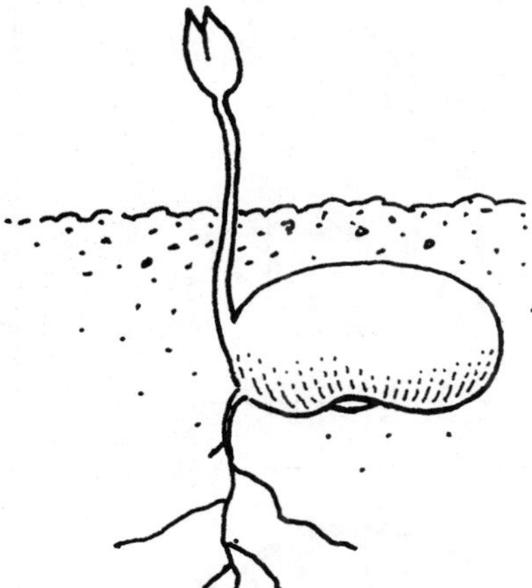

Name________________________ Date__________________

Hear and Write Long e

The letters **ea** can stand for the long **e** sound. Name each picture. If the name has the long **e** sound, write **ea** on the line.

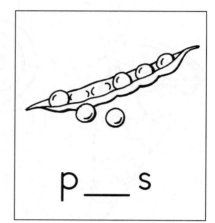

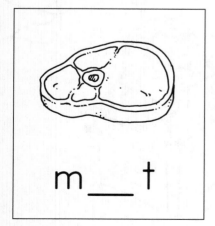

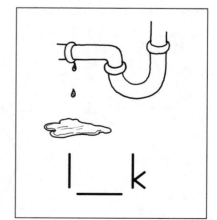

l___n

s___l

p___s

t___m

b___k

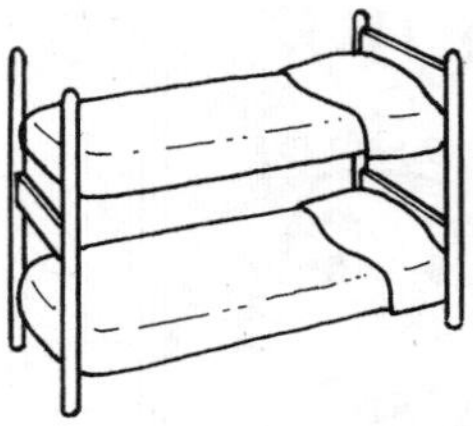

b___nk

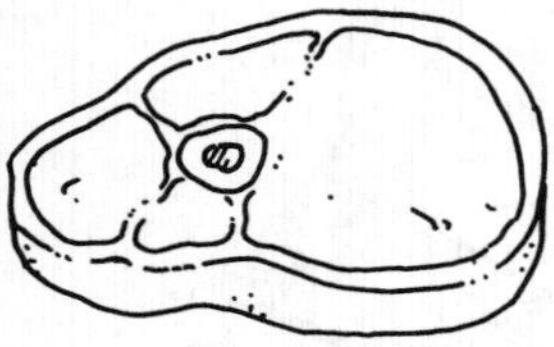

m___t

m___t

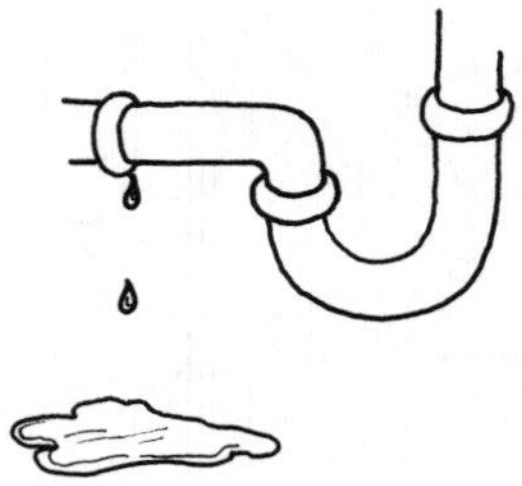

l___k

Name ____________________ Date ____________________

Hear and Write Long e

The letters **ee** can stand for the long **e** sound. Name each picture. If the name has the long **e** sound, write **ee** on the line.

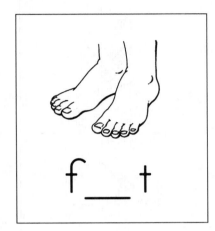

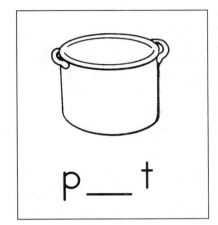

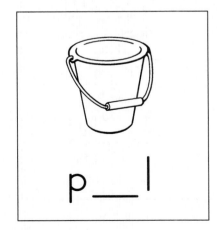

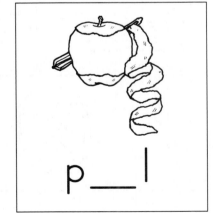

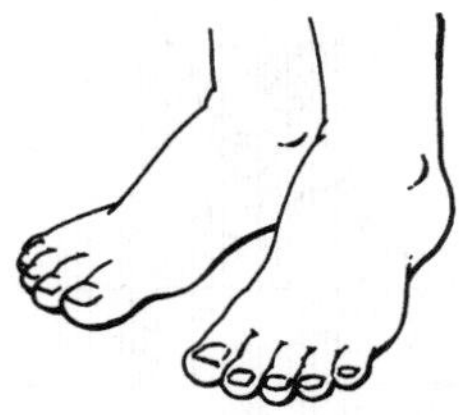

f___t

p___t

w___d

b___s

v___t

qu___n

p___l

p___l

sh___p

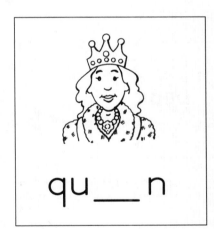

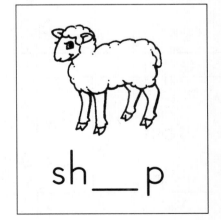

Name ______________________ Date ________________

Read and Rhyme 

Name each picture. Circle the pictures that rhyme with the word at the beginning of each row.

need	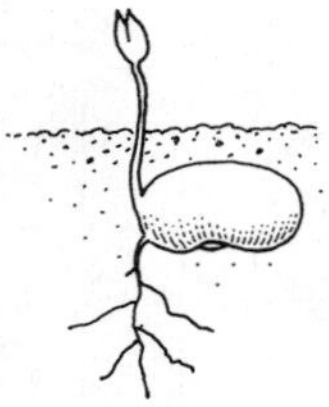		
beat		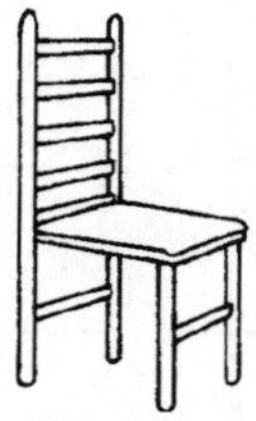	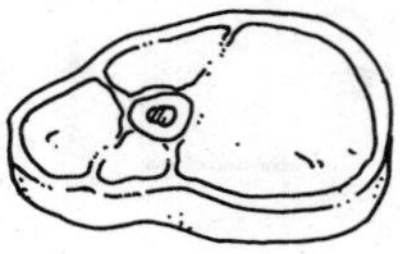
peak		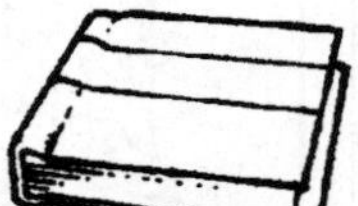	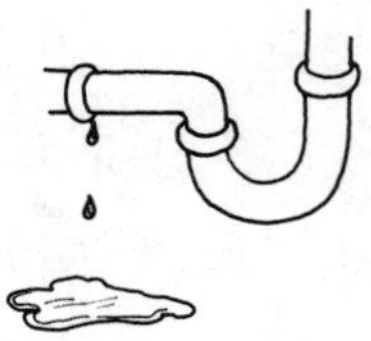
cream			
feel	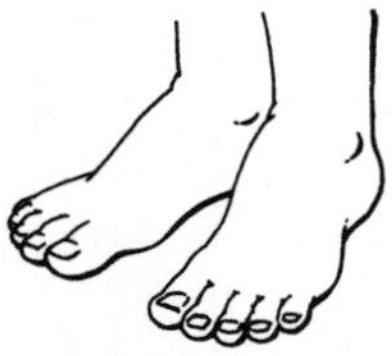		

Name ______________________ Date ________________

Sounds and Sentences

Circle the word with the long **e** sound that completes the sentence. Write it on the line.

1. The ______________ leave the hive.

bags
bones
bees

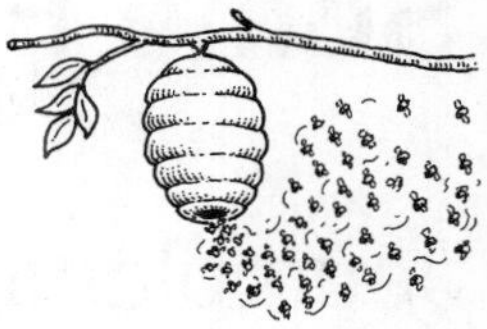

2. They ______________ on a rose.

meet
mule
mat

3. Pollen gets on their ______________.

fate
fit
feet

4. Pollen helps ______________ grow.

seeds
sides
sits

5. The bees rest on a ______________.

loaf
leaf
life

6. They make a fine ______________.

time
ten
team

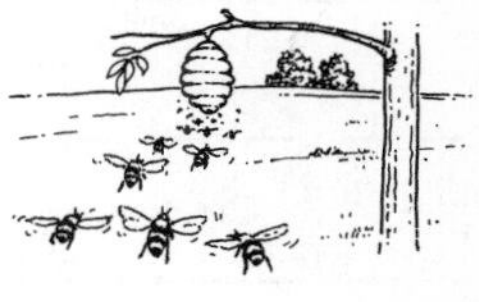

Name ______________________ Date ________________

Story Time

Read the story. Answer the question. Color the picture.

Some Fine Seeds

Jean plants seeds.
She gets out the hose.
The seeds need to get wet.
The seeds seem fine now.
Jean will get peas to eat.

Why did Jean plant seeds?

____

____

Name ______________________________ Date ______________________

Listen for the Vowel Sounds of y

The letter **y** can stand for the long **i** sound in **fly** or the long **e** sound in **baby**. Name each picture. If you hear the **y** sound in **fly**, color the picture blue. If you hear the **y** sound in **baby**, color the picture green.

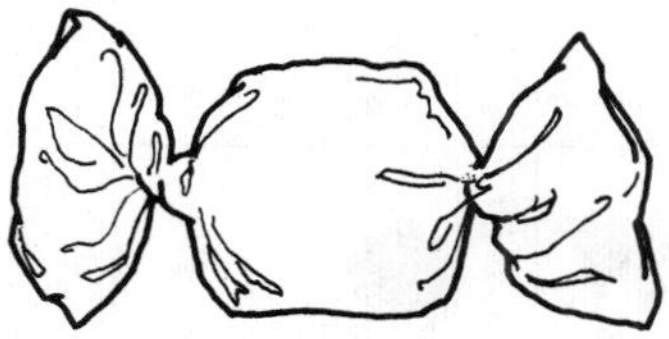

Name ______________________ Date ____________________

Read Vowel y Words

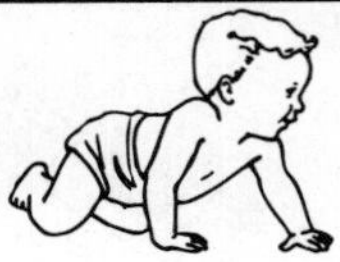

Name each picture. Circle the word that names the picture.

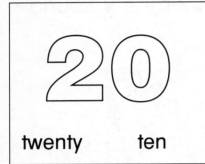

20

twenty ten

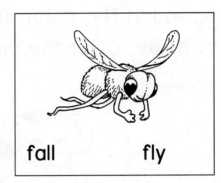

pea puppy

fall fly

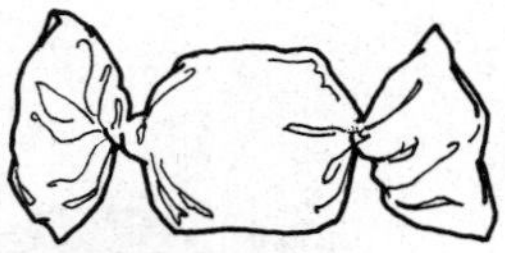

candy can

pine pony

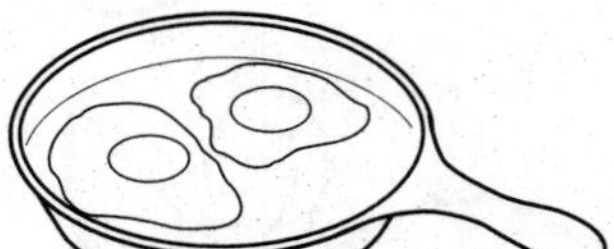

free fry

skate sky

cot cry

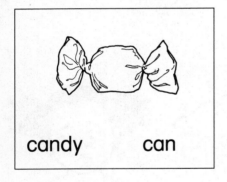

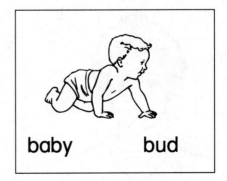

baby bud

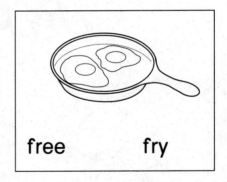

Name ______________________ Date ________________

Hear and Write Vowel y

Name each picture. If you hear the **y** sound in **fly**, write a red **y**. If you hear the **y** sound in **penny**, write a green **y**.

sk__

twent__

pon__

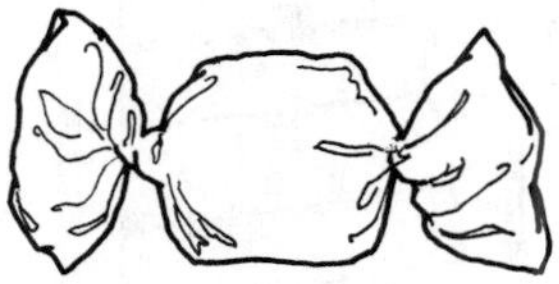

cand__

bunn__

pupp__

bab__

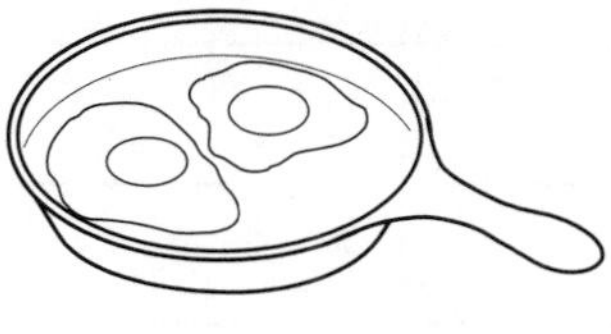

fr__

cr__

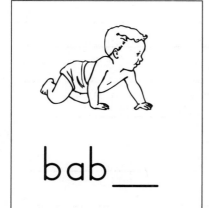

Name ______________________ Date ______________

Story Time

Read the story. Answer the questions. Color the picture.

Funny Pony

Lucy has a baby pony.
The pony is funny.
It likes to eat jelly.
It likes to eat candy.
Candy and jelly are not
healthy for a pony.
We feed apples to the pony.

What things does the pony like?

____

____

Why are they bad for the pony?

____

____

Lee Likes to Ride

____

made this book!

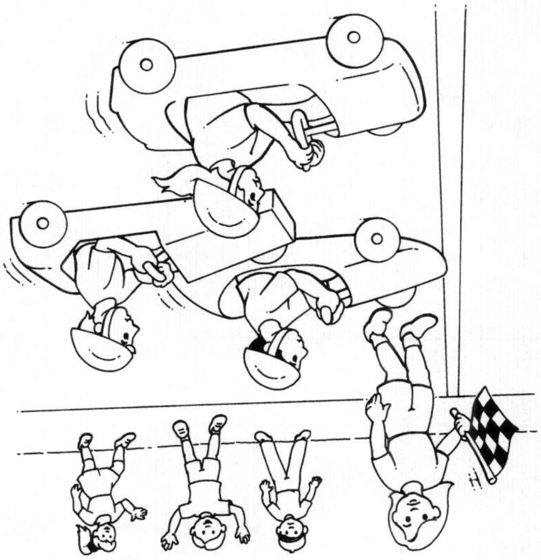

Lee sits at the wheel.
The cars take off.

Lee feels a huge bump.
It is not a real road. It is fun.

Do you like to ride?
Draw the ride you like best.

money

mask

milk

mouse

mitten

moon

map

24

m	m	
m		m
	m	m

25

d		d	d
d			d
d	d	d	

26

d	d	
	d	
d	d	d

27

fence

football

fish

five

fork

fire

feather

fox

28

f		f
	f	
		f

29

g	g	g	
g	g		g
	g	g	g

30

g	g	g
	g	
g	g	g

31

ball

butter

banana

bird

bench

basket

bat

bed

32

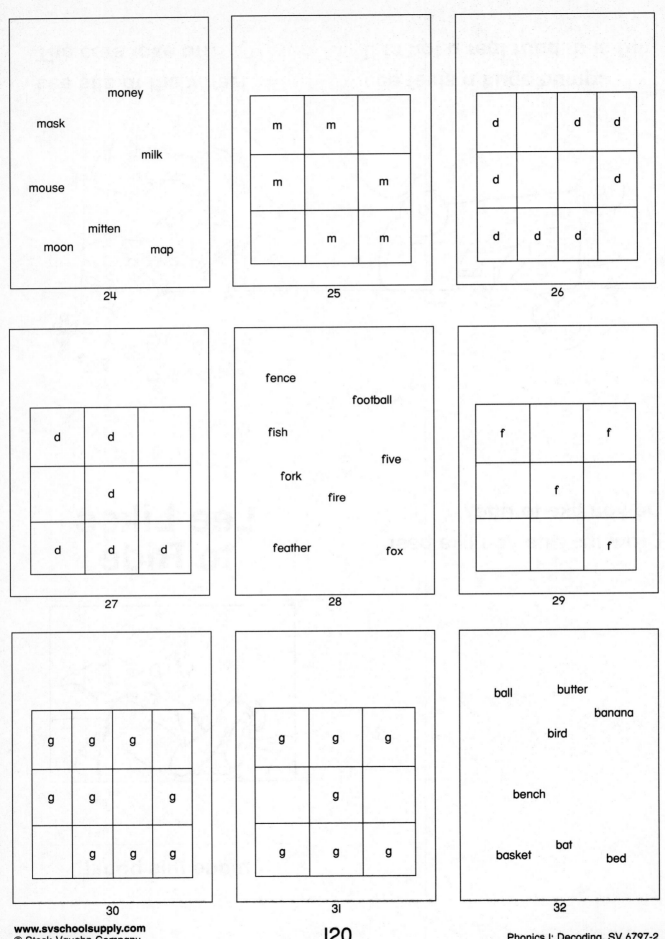

b	b	
b	b	b
	b	b

33

	t	t	t
t	t		t
	t	t	t

34

t	t	
t	t	t
	t	t

35

saddle
seal
sandwich
sink
saw
seven
salt
sun

36

s		s
	s	
s		s

37

w		w	w
	w	w	w
w	w	w	

38

king
kite
kitten
kick
kangaroo

39

k	k	
	k	k
k	k	

40

	j		j
	j	j	j
j		j	j

41

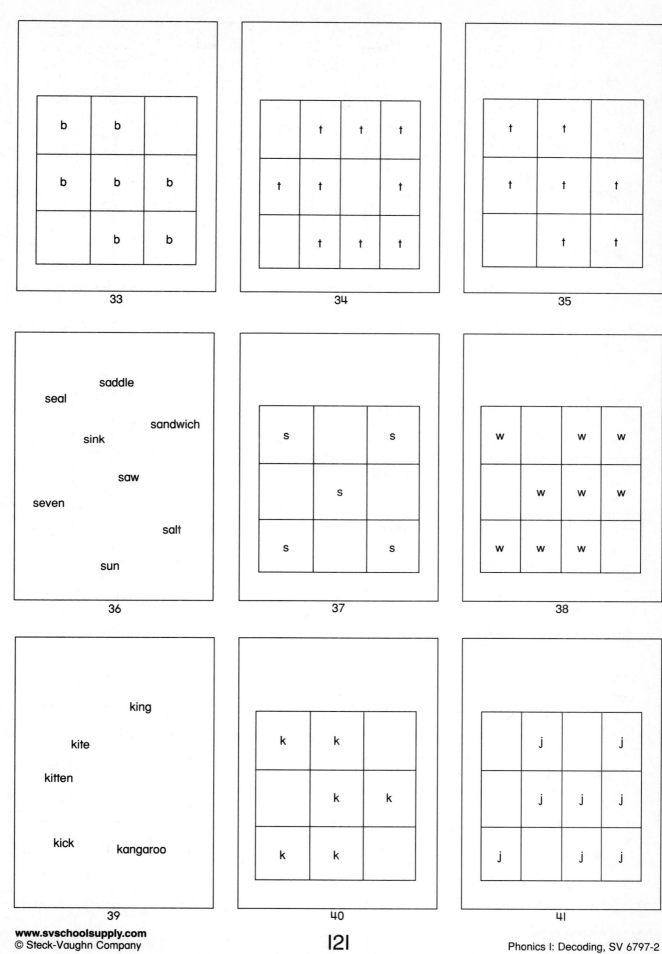

pitcher puppet
pineapple
pin
pencil
piano
pillow purse

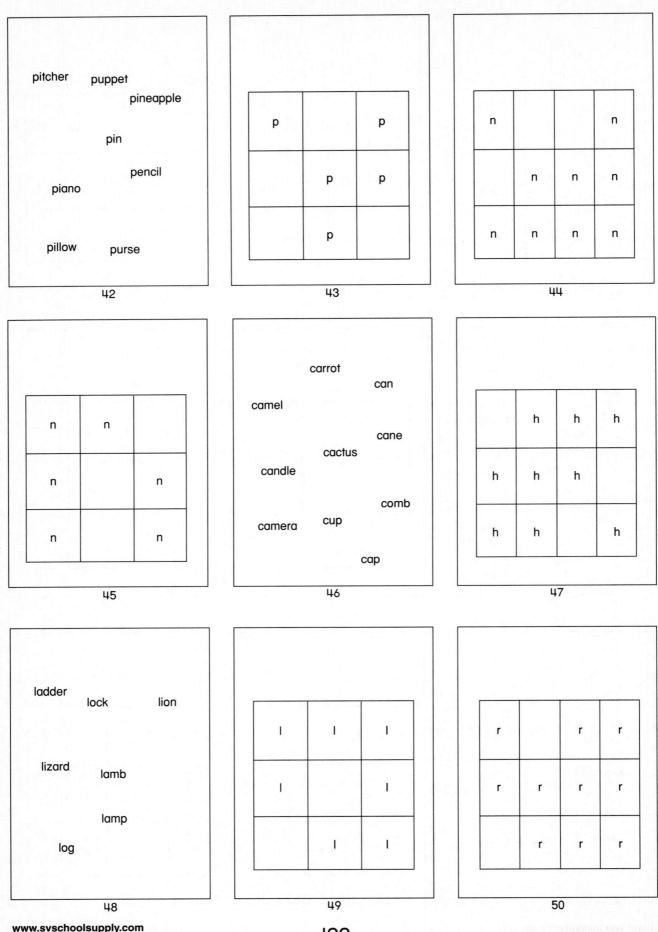

42

p		p
	p	p
	p	

43

n			n
	n	n	n
n	n	n	n

44

n	n	
n		n
n		n

45

carrot
can
camel
cane
cactus
candle
comb
camera cup
cap

46

	h	h	h
h	h	h	
h	h		h

47

ladder lock lion
lizard
lamb
lamp
log

48

l	l	l
l		l
	l	l

49

r		r	r
r	r	r	r
	r	r	r

50

r		r
r	r	r
r		r

51

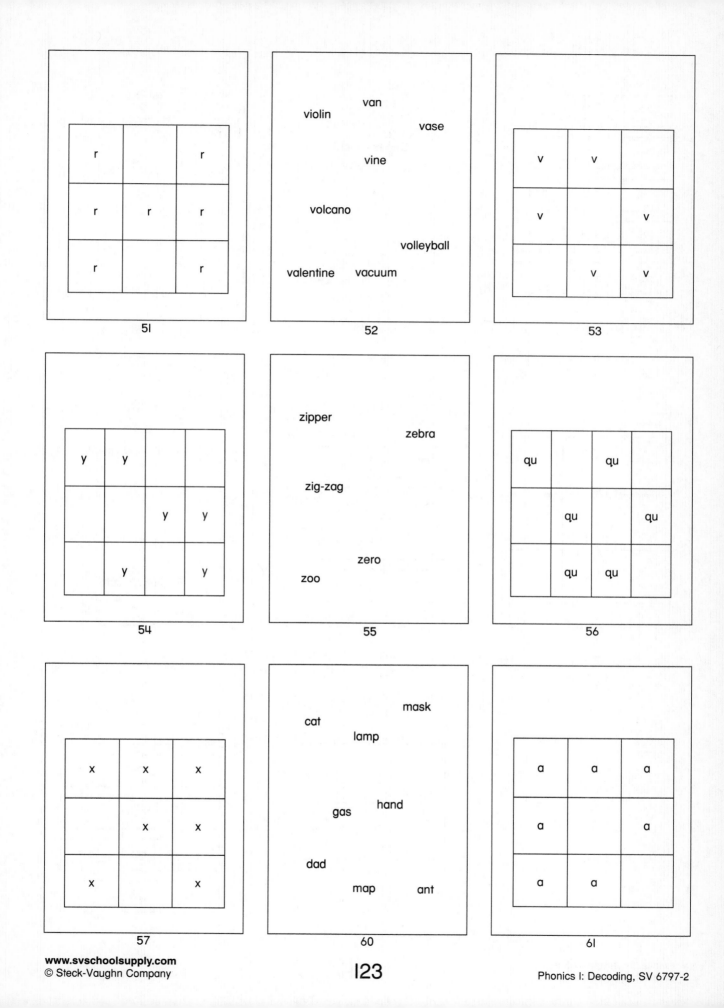

violin
van
vase
vine
volcano
volleyball
valentine
vacuum

52

v	v	
v		v
	v	v

53

y	y		
		y	y
	y		y

54

zipper
zebra
zig-zag
zero
zoo

55

qu		qu	
	qu		qu
	qu	qu	

56

x	x	x
	x	x
x		x

57

mask
cat
lamp
hand
gas
dad
map
ant

60

a	a	a
a		a
a	a	

61

jam dam

can fan

mad dad

hat mat

cap map

62

Dad has a hat.

The cat is in the hat.

63

zipper

chick

fish

pig

mix

mitt

ship

65

i		i
i	i	i
	i	i

66

pin fin

ship zip

spill hill

pig dig

hit pit

67

Kim can dig a big pit.

Bill has six cats.

68

fox

lock

box

doll

top

sock

blocks

70

	fox	top
cot	log	pop
pot	box	

71

frog dog

clock lock

mop top

cot pot

fox box

72

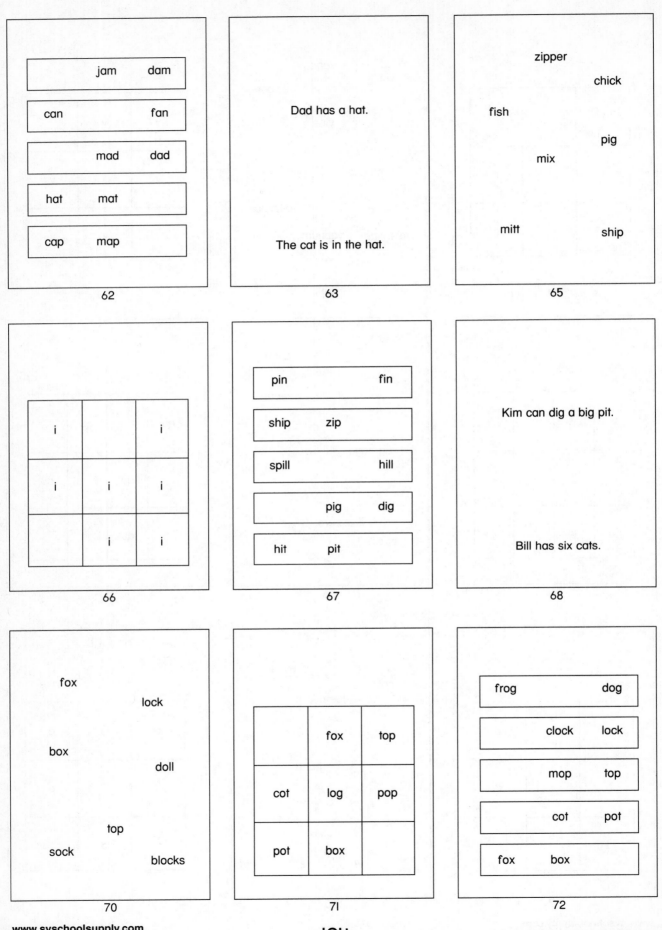

The fox jogs to the log.

The top is not in the box.

73

drum

brush

skunk

duck

plug

thumb

bunk

75

u		u
u	u	u
	u	u

76

run		sun
	plug	bug
	nut	cut
drum	gum	
cub		tub

77

The cub jumps at the bug.

The pup is in the tub.

78

ten

web

vest

nest

pen

check

bell

leg

80

	e	e
e	e	e
e		e

81

	bread	bed
pen		ten
well	bell	
vet		net
	leg	beg

82

The vet helps the pet.

Ken is all wet.

83

frame
tray
nail
cane
sail
lake

86

a e	a e	
a e		a e
	a e	a e

87

ai		ai
ai	ai	
	ai	ai

88

ay		ay
ay	ay	
ay		ay

89

cake rake

sail tail

jay hay

tape cape

tray day

90

cake

made

wait

pay

plate

take

91

dime
mice
bike
dive
kite
five
vine

93

i e	i e	
	i e	i e
i e	i e	

94

line nine

lime dime

mice dice

five dive

pine vine

95

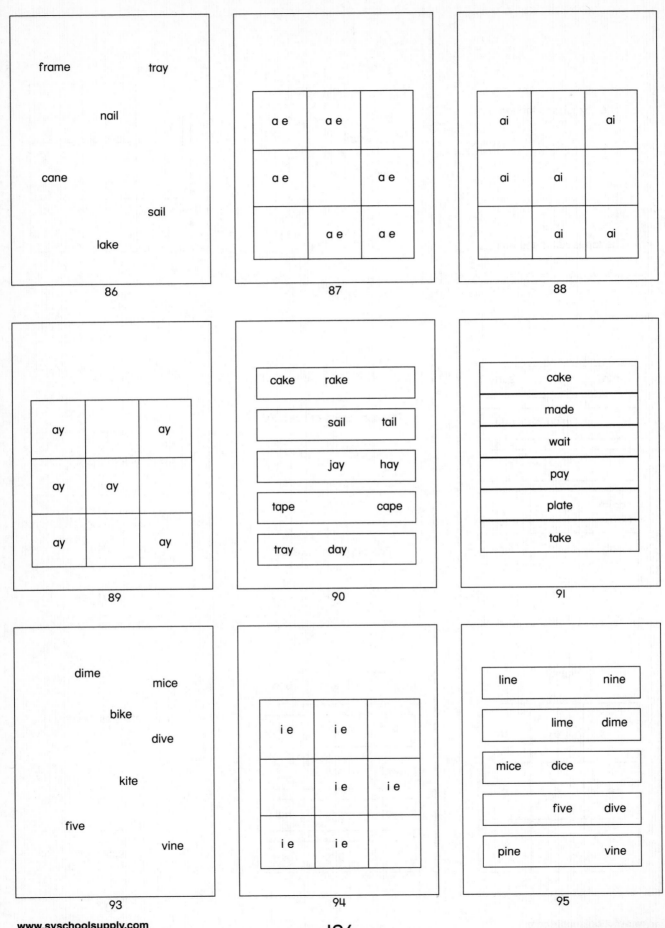

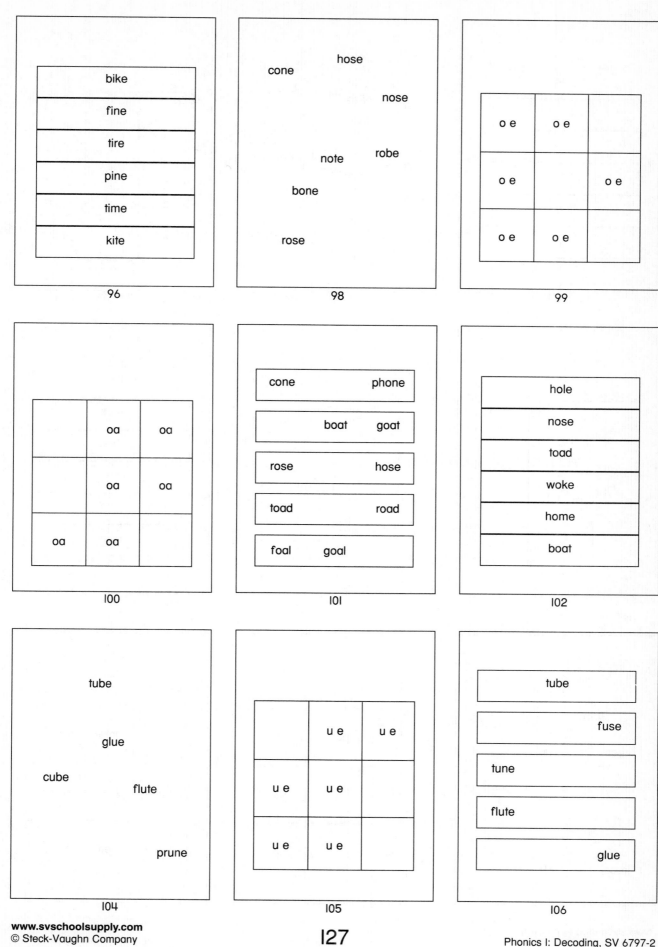

bike
fine
tire
pine
time
kite

96

cone hose nose note robe bone rose

98

o e	o e	
o e		o e
o e	o e	

99

	oa	oa
	oa	oa
oa	oa	

100

cone	phone
boat	goat
rose	hose
toad	road
foal	goal

101

hole
nose
toad
woke
home
boat

102

tube glue cube flute prune

104

	u e	u e
u e	u e	
u e	u e	

105

tube
fuse
tune
flute
glue

106

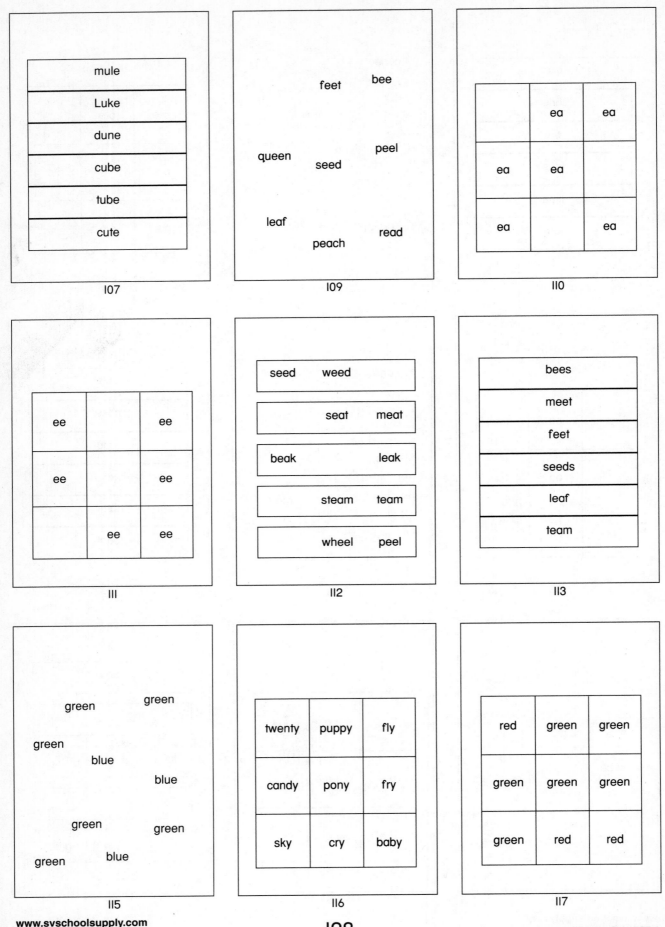

mule
Luke
dune
cube
tube
cute

107

feet bee

queen seed peel

leaf peach read

109

	ea	ea
ea	ea	
ea		ea

110

ee		ee
ee		ee
	ee	ee

111

seed	weed	
	seat	meat
beak		leak
	steam	team
	wheel	peel

112

bees
meet
feet
seeds
leaf
team

113

green green

green

blue

blue

green green

green blue

115

twenty	puppy	fly
candy	pony	fry
sky	cry	baby

116

red	green	green
green	green	green
green	red	red

117